STAFF RECOMMENDATIONS

P9-EJZ-345

**From a devoted reader and lifelong bookseller,
an eloquent and charming reflection on the
singular importance of bookstores**

Do we need bookstores in the twenty-first century?
If so, what makes a good one? In this beautifully
written book, Jeff Deutsch—the director of Chicago's
Seminary Co-op Bookstores, one of the finest bookstores in the world—pays loving tribute to one of our
most important and endangered civic institutions.
He considers how qualities like space, time, abundance, and community find expression in a good
bookstore. Along the way, he also predicts—perhaps
audaciously—a future in which the bookstore not
only endures, but realizes its highest aspirations.

In exploring why good bookstores matter, Deutsch
draws on his lifelong experience as a bookseller,
but also his upbringing as an Orthodox Jew. This
spiritual and cultural heritage instilled in him a
reverence for reading, not as a means to a living, but
as an essential part of a meaningful life. Central
among Deutsch's arguments for the necessity of
bookstores is the incalculable value of browsing—
since, when we are deep in the act of looking at the
shelves, we move through space as though we are
inside the mind itself, immersed in self-reflection.

In the age of one-click shopping, this is no ordi-
nary defense of bookstores, but rather an urgent account of why they are essential places of discovery,
refuge, and fulfillment that enrich the communities
that are lucky enough to have them.

"In this charming work, a revered bookseller puts into words the strong but often inarticulate feeling that many booklovers have about the importance of bookstores. Deutsch makes an eloquent case for the way bookstores educate readers as no classroom or library can. His wide-ranging reflections teach us to value the bookstore as a site not of goods but of experiences."

—LEAH PRICE, author of *What We Talk about When We Talk about Books*

"A compendium of delights for the thoughtful reader. Deutsch, a gifted writer and riveting storyteller, has written a concisely elegant topography of the good bookstore that also illuminates the seemingly opaque craft of bookselling. This book is bound to be the fulcrum of discussions—among readers, booksellers, editors, and publishers—about the meaning and role of bookstores."

—PAUL YAMAZAKI, City Lights Bookstore

"A promiscuously erudite love letter to bookstores, books, readers, writers, and the unique community that they constitute, Deutsch's hypnotic book is generously laced with memorable and often hilarious quotations, and offers the exquisite pleasures of browsing through the book-lined mind of an omnivorously literate reader and bookseller."

—WENDY DONIGER, author of *The Hindus*

"Maintaining an open society requires educated citizens, book culture, and bookstores, one of the few truly democratic institutions, open to all. Infused with a deep love of his profession, bookselling, Jeff Deutsch's reflection on reading, learning, and well-run bookstores is breathtaking. Read and share this compelling and engaging book."

—HAKI R. MADHUBUTI, founder of Third World Press and author of *Taught by Women: Poems as Resistance Language*

IN PRAISE OF GOOD BOOKSTORES

In Praise
of Good
Bookstores

JEFF DEUTSCH

PRINCETON UNIVERSITY PRESS
PRINCETON & OXFORD

Published by Princeton University Press
41 William Street, Princeton, New Jersey 08540
99 Banbury Road, Oxford OX2 6JX

press.princeton.edu

All Rights Reserved

Library of Congress Cataloging-in-Publication Data

Names: Deutsch, Jeff, [Date]– author.
Title: In praise of good bookstores / Jeff Deutsch. Description: Princeton : Princeton University Press, 2022. | Includes bibliographical references and index.
Identifiers: LCCN 2021040299 (print) | LCCN 2021040300 (ebook) | ISBN 9780691207766 (hardback) | ISBN 9780691229669 (ebook)
Subjects: LCSH: Booksellers and bookselling—United States—History—20th century. | Booksellers and bookselling—United States—History—21st century. | Bookstores—Social aspects. | Books and reading—Social aspects. | Seminary Co-op Bookstores, Inc. | Deutsch, Jeff, [Date]– | LCGFT: Essays.
Classification: LCC Z473 .D48 2022 (print) | LCC Z473 (ebook) | DDC 341/.4500209730904—dc23
LC record available at https://lccn.loc.gov/2021040299
LC ebook record available at https://lccn.loc.gov/2021040300

British Library Cataloging-in-Publication Data is available

Editorial: Rob Tempio and Matt Rohal
Production Editorial: Sara Lerner
Text and Cover Design: Chris Ferrante
Production: Erin Suydam
Publicity: Maria Whelan and Kate Farquhar-Thomson
Copyeditor: Cynthia Buck

Cover and endpaper illustrations by Aimee David

This book has been composed in Bookman Old Style and Job Clarendon

Printed on acid-free paper. ∞

Printed in the United States of America

10 9 8 7 6 5 4 3 2 1

*To the booksellers past, present, and future who
humbly and quietly distinguish this profession*

*To Linda, Haskell, and Erica, whose bookishness
and love provided the model*

*To May, that brilliant bookseller, whose love is the
greatest gift I ever received from bookselling*

And similarly we all have ready to our access in the bookshop, one of the greatest instruments of civilization; and yet none of us—neither publishers, booksellers, nor customers—have yet learned more than an inkling of what that place can accomplish.

—CHRISTOPHER MORLEY

No man, therefore, can serve both books and Mammon.

—RICHARD DE BURY

You already belong to your time.

—LYDIA DAVIS

CONTENTS

The Presence of Books: An Introduction............... 1

CHAPTER ONE. Space 19

CHAPTER TWO. Abundance 50

CHAPTER THREE. Value 78

CHAPTER FOUR. Community 109

CHAPTER FIVE. Time.. 137

The Good Bookstore: An Epilogue..................... 162

Acknowledgments 169

Notes 173

Bibliography 183

Index 191

IN PRAISE OF GOOD BOOKSTORES

The Presence of Books

AN INTRODUCTION

Let Your enormous Library be justified.
—JORGE LUIS BORGES, "The Library of Babel"

THE RARE PUBLICAN

The sociologist Edward Shils wrote, "It may well be that we live in an epoch in which the bookshop is an institution suspended between 'the dying old society' and the 'society struggling to be born.'"[1] Would that we were living in an epoch in which the bookshop itself was so clearly the given, as it was in Shils's.

Throughout the centuries, we booksellers have looked back on a more genteel or refined era, when the business of selling quality books to serious general readers was viable. But our nostalgia, like much nostalgia, is likely fictive, or at least imprecise; good bookstores have never made good business sense. We know from Shils's 1963 essay "The Bookshop in America" that the difficulty of maintaining good bookstores isn't new, but in our time it has become ever more acute, as the society struggling to be born might well leave the bookstores behind altogether if

I

we don't develop a model that supports what is best in them.

Shils was a particularly eloquent practitioner of a genre: the lamentation of the state of bookselling in our time. Speaking to the newly formed Booksellers' League in 1895, its president, Charles T. Dillingham, remarked upon "the gradual decrease in the number of retail booksellers as a distinct class," noting that "there are few left of the species outside the large cities."[2] As far back as the eighteenth century, in their *Encyclopédie*'s entry for bookselling, Denis Diderot and Jean le Rond d'Alembert included the complaint "that Bookselling is no longer worth anything, that the book trade is no longer going well."[3]

We don't need another lamentation of the state of bookselling in our time, but I do think that, before it's too late, we would be wise to consider a certain ideal of bookselling—that we imagine a future in which bookstores not only endure but realize their highest aspirations.

In 1994, there were approximately 7,000 independent bookstores in the United States.[4] As of 2019, there were 2,500, and of those few bookstores left, even fewer sell books exclusively.[5] Neither of these facts is incidental. In the twenty-first century, readers no longer need bookstores to buy books. Furthermore, from a retail perspective, the net profit from book sales alone is not sufficient to support bookselling as a financial endeavor.

Why do we even need bookstores at all then? And presuming we do, how can we build a model that supports them, that allows them to serve their highest ideals?

• • •

What a strange thing, the bookshop. There are just *so many* books. In 2019, there were 20 million published books available, not counting books published that year. Every book requires considerable attention to write, publish, sell, and read. Books serve such diverse purposes and are written for so few readers at a given time. As such, efficiencies common to other industries are impossible in the book industry.

The remarkable and perhaps unique thing about the good bookstore is that it has never counted on the blockbuster—or what Shils describes as "overstuffed political books" and "puffy and pallid biographies"—to thrive, but on thousands and thousands of singular "products" (forgive me, booksellers) that must be patiently left on the shelves, rendering capital inert, as it were, until their destined reader discovers them.[6]

John Ruskin, the nineteenth-century art critic and armchair political economist, in his 1891 lecture "Sesame and Lilies," writes of "books of the hour" and "books of all time," noting, of course, that this isn't a distinction of quality—there are good and bad books of the hour and good and bad books of all time—but of species. If the conventional wisdom is to be believed, there are books of the hour that one must read in order to participate in the cultural conversation and books of all time that everyone is meant to have read. This is not the case, of course, and that is one of the great virtues of the book trade and the reading public. Surely there are books of either category that enough people have read that it *seems* like everyone is reading them—or has already read them—but we booksellers know that the conventional wisdom is false and has little bearing on the work of bookselling. The bookstore is a haven for the heterodox.

The good bookstore's collection comprises books that might have been published a month ago, a year ago, a half-century ago, a couple of millennia ago; the attuned bookseller must provide a selection of books of all vintages. To do so, the work of bookselling demands a firm grasp not just of the literature of the ages but also of the literature of one's lifetime and of the thousands of new publications announced in the publishers' catalogs that arrive seasonally, and by the dozens. Only a minute fraction of the books one considers will make the shelves. Discernment is the primary quality of the good bookseller; filtration, selection, assemblage, and enthusiasm their work.

As a business proposition, this model is clearly untenable. No retailer, whose work is to buy cheap and sell dear, would develop the business of the bookstore. The newspaperman H. L. Mencken, speaking to the same point in his 1930 essay "Lo, the Poor Bookseller," writes:

> The marvel is, indeed, that [the bookseller] ever survives at all. It is as if a haberdasher, in addition to meeting all the hazards of the current fashion,

had to keep in stock a specimen of every kind of shirt, collar, sock, necktie and undershirt in favor since 1750.[7]

Ninety-odd years later, our conundrum hasn't changed, even if the books and authors have. Our customers might find our stock insufficient if we don't offer the latest Ta-Nehisi Coates or Elena Ferrante, while another, less contemporary, reader might be disappointed by not finding twenty-five-year-old volumes by bell hooks or Elizabeth Hardwick. And that same bookseller must know which Coates and which Ferrante, if any, to keep on the shelf and which, if any, to let go a decade from now.

On these points, the novelist and enthusiast on behalf of bookstores Christopher Morley, writing at the same time as Mencken, understood our challenge well. The bookseller, he writes, "has to combine the functions of the bar-room and the bodega. He must be able to serve, on demand, not only the cocktail of the moment but also the scarcest of old vintages. How rare is the publican who understands the merits of both."[8]

It's clear that the *business* of bookselling is secondary for most booksellers, which is why they find creative ways to make profits elsewhere, that they might continue to sell the sorts of books that drew them to the work in the first place. Most of them, too, would expect to see the likes of Coates, Ferrante, hooks, and Hardwick on the shelves of any good bookstore. In our time, bookstores have taken to selling everything from socks to coffee, just as booksellers in Shils's time took to "dealing in pen-wipers, blotters, writing pads, and greeting cards or gramophone discs," and of course we understand why: they need the margin.[9]

I have been a bookseller since 1994, and throughout my career I have operated these sorts of stores. The pull of the presence of books is so strong that I have, without pride but without shame, supplemented the book collection with notebooks, coffee, greeting cards, and other sidelines, thinking it a reasonable compromise to maintain a decent bookstore. And it is. Even decent bookstores, I would argue, are tremendously important to a thriving community. But they aren't representative of our highest aspirations.

Neither, of course, is the largest and most mercenary seller of books in the world, Amazon. In fact, the *work* of bookselling is completely circumvented. This twenty-first-century model of selling books is an "everything store" that does away with filtration, selection, assemblage, and enthusiasm entirely. Jeff Bezos, in a talk delivered to the Special Libraries Conference in 1997, explained that he chose books as the first product his new company would sell because "there are more items in the book category than there are items in any other category by far."[10] In addition, their relatively uniform size made them easy to package and ship. That Bezos then turned books into loss leaders (products sold at a loss in order to attract customers who will then purchase higher-margin products, creating profitable transactions) is particularly unsavory considering that professional booksellers have long placed a higher value on their cultural work than on the tremendous effort required to achieve even thin margins selling books. They *needed* to sell socks in order to make bookselling profitable; Bezos *chose* to devalue books in order to make already profitable merchandise, like socks, even more profitable.

But, lest we give ourselves over to lamentation, let's consider a different sort of bookstore.

DISLODGING SHADES

In 1961, two years before Shils published "The Bookshop in America," five students of the Chicago Theological Seminary established a consumer cooperative whose purpose was

> to make available, primarily to students, faculty members and administrative officers of theological seminaries and other scholastic institutions located at or near the campus of the University of Chicago . . . books, publications and supplies used in the study of theology and for building up by such persons, seminaries or institutions of their professional and scholarly libraries.

The second article of incorporation reads in full, "The name of the association is the Seminary Cooperative Bookstore, Inc."[11]

Shils was a member of the University of Chicago's faculty in 1961, holding joint appointments in the Sociology Department and on the Committee on Social Thought. Perhaps the early booksellers of the Seminary Co-op read Shils's essay. In 1969, the general manager of the Co-op, John Modschiedler, hired Jack Cella, who began his forty-year tenure as the leader of the Co-op in 1973. There is little doubt that Shils expressed his opinions to the seven shopkeeps running the bookstores in Hyde Park, including Cella. Shils had a reputation for many things, but timidity expressing his opinions on matters of the intellect was certainly not one. Even if they hadn't read the essay, they probably heard Shils express his anathemas in their shops. In 1978, Shils became the 8,704[th] member of the Co-op.

As bookselling in general is an unlikely, and perhaps unwise, business, serious bookselling must be an extraordinarily foolish financial endeavor. "Why should anyone who has or who can obtain $10,000 or $20,000," asks Shils, "invest it in a bookshop to sell serious books when, if he were an economically reasonable person, he would do better to open a beauty parlor or a hamburger and barbecue shop, or put his money into the stock market?"[12] Shils's question is rhetorical—he knew why. Cella and Modschiedler knew why. If the aim of a reasonable person is to live a life of meaning and purpose, serious books can provide the concentrate of the examined life.

In the last three decades of the twentieth century, Cella and the legion of booksellers who worked beside him built arguably the best serious bookstore in America. They ignored the incredibly specific purpose for which the bookstore was established and built an expansive institution. Good bookstores reflect their communities; exceptional bookstores both reflect and create their communities. In those early years, the Seminary Co-op did both superbly.

Upon Cella's retirement in 2013, the philosopher Jonathan Lear, a longtime Co-op member, wondered about his successor. "Where does one post the help-wanted ad: Looking for a soul (or souls) willing to be incarnate in a bookstore?"[13]

• • •

Sometimes the mere existence of a phenomenon—a human, an institution, a work of art—is worthy of awe. Its declaration cannot be countermanded. When I first descended the perilous staircase leading to the old Co-op in 1994—incidentally, the year Amazon was founded—the bookstore was in its heyday. Like many who came before and after me, I was deeply persuaded by the Seminary Co-op's existence. The bookstore was a realization of a humble but powerful vision: a broad selection of books whose presence on the shelves created an unparalleled browsing experience undiluted by tchotchkes or knickknacks, pen wipers or gramophone discs, and only the occasional puffy or pallid volume. The collection created a totalizing environment; engagement with this landscape of book spines shifted the patron's sense of space, time, abundance, value, and community. To a confused and restless young man trying to find his way in the world, who knew only that the presence of books was of paramount importance, the Co-op seemed as close to a spiritual home as he could hope to find.

It was, in fact, a religion predicated upon books from which I was attempting to take my leave. But even then I knew that, whatever else was left behind, the presence of books would remain.

I grew up in an Orthodox Jewish community in and around Brooklyn. The rooms of my childhood in Flatbush, Boro Park, and Elizabeth, New Jersey, were all book-lined; my childhood homes, my yeshiva, my shul, my relatives' homes, and the homes of my friends' families were heavy with large books.

From 1957 until 2012, my grandparents lived in a second-floor walkup apartment that they rented in Boro Park, on the corner of Sixteenth Avenue and Fifty-Third Street. My grandfather's library—or rather, book-lined living room—made a particular impression. The bookcases were filled with books whose gravity was clear from the ornate, uniform spines. Ornate these books, but not ornamental. The bookshelves always had gaps, and the gaps would move from week to week; an ever-rotating selection of volumes would be laid out on my grandfather's bookstand and desk.

These books were read—books are for use, after all—and were treated with reverence and love. Observant Jews are accustomed to kissing the cover of a book after closing it—a habit that has remained with me throughout the years. Along with the British literatus Leigh Hunt, who, in effusing about books, wrote of how he liked to lean his head against them, followers of my given tradition might say, "When I speak of being in contact with my books, I mean it literally."[14]

These books were read in groups called *chevrusas*, a Hebrew word whose root means "friend." When I was a young boy, I would join my grandfather's *chevrusa* on occasion, just to observe. Seated on an austere bench in the basement of the shul across the street, my head barely clearing the tabletop, I sat with large men and their large Aramaic books watching them question, ponder, argue with, and delight in what they found on those pages.

My grandfather wasn't a scholar. He was a shopkeep. He ran a suit store named Chatham Clothes on New Utrecht Avenue, selling kosher clothing to the *haredi* Jews in the tri-state area. He worked long days, after which he would eat dinner with his family before heading across the street to learn with his *chevrusa*.

The activity called "learning" was common. Because there was only one thing to study—the Tanach and its many commentaries, especially the Talmud—there was no need to specify the object of learning. Learning was a daily activity, regardless of one's age, and was no less special for being an everyday endeavor. And learning, while it reliably yielded wisdom and pleasure, was understood to be an end in itself.

The highest compliment one could pay in that community was to say that someone was learned, or a *talmid chacham*, a wise student. When, as a teenager, I moved into the secular world, I found some of the conventions around books and education profoundly alien. I couldn't fathom the notion that one strove to become educated rather than learned, or that one might study in order to make a living, rather than to learn, continually, an endeavor essential to living a more meaningful life. What, after all, was the point of making a living if not to build community and create deeper understanding—to come home for dinner and then learn with one's *chevrusa*?

• • •

The Chicago poet Nate Marshall once said, during an event at the Co-op, that "the greatest thing a poet or poem can give you is permission." A bookstore too, it turns out, can give you permission. That is precisely what that first descent into the Co-op established: permission to be among books outside of an institution of learning, be it a university or a yeshiva, and outside of a teleological paradigm.

I remember how awestruck I was on that first descent. It recalled the British essayist Charles Lamb's remembrances of his first engagement with the library at Oxford:

What a place to be in is an old library! It seems as though all the souls of all the writers, that have bequeathed their labors to these Bodleians, were reposing here, as in some dormitory, or middle state. I do not want to handle, to profane the leaves, their winding-sheets. I could as soon dislodge a shade. I seem to inhale learning, walking amid their foliage; and the odor of their old moth-scented coverings is fragrant as the first bloom of those sciential apples which grew amid the happy orchard.[15]

Following my grandfather's model—books aren't ornaments—and knowing that there were treasures to be found within the volumes, I quickly became fearless in dislodging shades. As my intellectual life was developed in the interstices between the yeshiva and the academy, the justification of the existence of a bookstore like the Seminary Co-op was self-evident. This was the place where one could become learned—a *talmid chacham*—and fashion a daily practice that would lead one through a more meaningful life.

The philosopher Francis Bacon's musings on "the pleasure and delight of knowledge and learning" would not have been out of place in the Talmud. "We see in all other pleasures," he writes with the perspicacity of one of the rabbinic fathers,

> there is satiety, and after they be used, their verdure departeth, which showeth well they be but deceits of pleasure, and not pleasures; and that it was the novelty which pleased, and not the quality. And, therefore, we see that voluptuous men turn

friars, and ambitious princes turn melancholy. But of knowledge there is no satiety, but satisfaction and appetite are perpetually interchangeable.[16]

The best parts of the tradition in which I was raised valued not only what endures but also meaningful ephemera, what the philosopher Simone Weil gestures toward in writing, "Stars and blossoming fruit trees: utter permanence and extreme fragility give one an equal sense of eternity."[17] It sought pleasures, not the deceits of pleasures. It sought to feed appetites whose satiety led to a satisfaction that endured and led to an appetite for further meaning, knowledge, and love—a pleasure whose verdure remains.

SOULS INCARNATE IN A BOOKSTORE

In 2014, I answered Lear's help-wanted ad and succeeded Cella at the helm of the Seminary Co-op. Since then, more than a dozen of the country's finest professional booksellers have joined me in this work. We "souls incarnate in a bookstore" quickly understood how difficult it is to articulate the experience of browsing the stacks of the Co-op, much less its value, to those who, by dint of distance or assumption, have not yet entered its hallowed space.

Having spent over seven years in the Seminary Co-op, and the prior twenty years in wonderfully large and serious bookstores throughout the country, I feel the pity of Heinsius for the ones "that know not this happiness." Heinsius, the keeper of the library at Leyden who, according to the great seventeenth-century melancholist Robert Burton, "was mewed up in it all the year long," is my kin.

> I no sooner . . . come into the library, but I bolt the door to me, excluding lust, ambition, avarice, and all such vices, whose nurse is idleness, the mother of ignorance, and Melancholy herself, and in the very lap of eternity, amongst so many divine souls, I take my seat, with so lofty a spirit and sweet content.[18]

I can't but effuse on behalf of this experience, this pleasure that, relying for satisfaction not on novelty but on quality, beckons us to return before too long. Booksellers are professional enthusiasts, and I hope the sharing of enthusiasm on behalf of individual books, honed so finely over a quarter-century of bookselling, will serve me well as I turn that enthusiasm toward the bookstore itself, exhorting you to join me as we articulate the need for the bookstore in the twenty-first century.

It is not just bookstores that I hope to celebrate, but the profession of bookselling as well. Dillingham, writing in 1895, speaks accurately to our current condition when he says that "bookselling has often been classed as next to a profession."[19] Shils says that the "desire to be a bookseller is not highly correlated with being a great reader,"[20] but this reveals an ignorance of the sort of reading at which the bookseller excels. The French philosopher Jean-Luc Nancy understands the bookseller to be a "transcendental reader: she provides her clients with the conditions of possibility for reading." He continues:

> A bookseller's customers are readers of reading at the same time as they are readers of the books they buy. The bookseller's reading doesn't only or simply consist in deciphering all the pages of every book; it is also a *lectio* as *election*, a choice, selection, or gleaning of ideas from books that are proposed as a function of the Idea that bookseller has both of the book and of reading, both of readers and of publishers. In that sense, current usage doesn't call the bookseller a book merchant. . . . Let's say, with less ambiguity, that the bookseller is one who delivers books [*un levreur de livres*].[21]

A simple and direct justification of bookstores no longer holds. We no longer *need* bookstores to buy books, even serious books. In fact, bookstores might well be an inefficient and inconvenient way to buy books in the twenty-first century, and it is certainly the case that we have become creatures of efficiency and convenience.

But efficiency is an inconsistent ideal, a dubious virtue. In fact, there are wise inefficiencies, as any artist or parent can attest. Like the readers they serve, booksellers embrace the inefficient elements of the bookstore, understanding that they are anything but wasteful. Given that they are not only deliberate but critical to creating a good bookstore, the time has come to no longer apologize for the inefficiencies inherent in good bookselling. The inherited model of retail, with which bookstores were established, is insufficient. We must recognize and then rectify the considerable devaluing of the work of booksellers in building spaces that contribute to a more learned, more understanding, and more fulfilled populace.

• • •

If we no longer need bookstores to buy books, why, then, do we still need bookstores? And what, in the twenty-first century, makes a good bookshop? Whatever answer we provide must begin with the presence of books and the impulse to browse those books; the best argument on behalf of bookstores is the bookstores themselves, carefully built by booksellers who, like Cella and our precursors, created an improbable place whose sheer existence provided a value to their bookish communities that far exceeded their financial dividends.

Join me as we make our way through the bookstore. I will use the bookstore itself—in many cases, the Seminary Co-op, although the experiences I describe are common to good bookstores—to make a case that a good bookshop, as Shils wrote, is "a necessary part of the habitat of a lively intelligence in touch with the world."[22] We will wander the stacks, pull a volume from the shelves, consider a thought or two, delight in a particularly felicitous observation,

daydream a bit, and hope to circumscribe the problem, that we might tighten the circumference around
the solution. As Walt Whitman says, "I and mine do
not convince by arguments, similes, rhymes; we convince by our presence."[23] So it might be with books;
so it might be with bookstores.

This book is not a lamentation (we have enough of
those!) but a celebration—and, perhaps incidentally,
a justification—of the good bookstore. To borrow from
Borges, I submit these thoughts that we might let our
enormous bookstore be justified.

• • • •

My grandmother gave up the apartment in Boro Park
in late 2012, eighteen years after the death of my
grandfather, and the same year the Seminary Co-op
moved one block east, from its subterranean origins
to an illuminated, but still humble, building adjacent
to Frank Lloyd Wright's Robie House. After her death
the following year, my grandparents' apartment was
razed. I had a chance to visit prior to the building's
demolition. As I climbed the staircase and entered
the vacated apartment, I was struck by the indentation in the carpet along the living room wall. My
grandfather's books had made their impermanent
mark and, for the better part of an hour, I beheld that
indentation, formed in space by weight and time, as
though I was considering the stars and the blossoming fruit trees, reflecting upon that which remains
and that which passes.

CHAPTER ONE
Space

Let attention be paid not to the matter, but to the shape I give it.
—MONTAIGNE, "Of Books,"
in *The Complete Essays of Montaigne*, 296

UNPURSUED APPOSITION

In a virtual age, the corporeality of the Seminary Co-op matters, even if, like many a legend, it has transcended its corporeal state. The Seminary Co-op is an idea, but it began in a place. It was a cooperative in the basement of a seminary. It is no longer a cooperative, and it is no longer in the basement of a seminary. Today the Seminary Co-op is housed in one of the least remarkable buildings in the architecturally rich Hyde Park neighborhood of Chicago. Perhaps this setting might one day be part of its charm, just as exposed pipes, low ceilings, and a decidedly humble portal became part of its charm during its first half-century.

Moving a fifty-year-old bookstore, already established as one of the finest serious bookstores in the world, presented an opportunity to rebuild deliberately what had first developed organically in response to the limits of space more than through intentional design. While few would deny the old space its magical quality, we patrons remember its impracticalities well: the treacherous stairwell, the menacing low pipes, the dreadful stuffiness, and the bag check necessitated by the cramped aisles (although many remember the clothespin markers with fondness). We would do well to remember that while the Seminary building is majestic, the basement itself has always been plain.

Gaston Bachelard, the French topoanalyst, in his stirring book *The Poetics of Space*, investigated the imagined values of what he called "felicitous space." Seeking to determine the value of "the space we love," he writes, "Space that has been seized upon by the imagination cannot remain indifferent space subject to the measures and estimates of the surveyor. It has been lived in . . . with all the partiality of the imagination."[1]

When it became clear that the Seminary Co-op needed to move out of the Chicago Theological Seminary, Cella and the Co-op's community pondered the qualities necessary for housing a world-class serious bookstore. They knew it needed to be a space devoted to books only. They knew that browsing was the primary activity the space would be meant to support and that the browsers' ability to lose themselves would be of paramount importance.

In designing the new Seminary Co-op, the architect Stanley Tigerman was responsible for solving these twin problems. Tigerman, recognizing the power of disorientation in browsing, attempted to re-create deliberately the original store's accidental architecture, built as it was in a space that no architect or interior designer (or fire marshal, for that matter) would ever imagine into a bookstore. To hear him tell it, the idea of the Co-op necessitated conditions that would confuse patrons and cause them to get lost in the stacks.

There was an uncertainty and an imperfection present in the old Co-op, reflective of the uncertainty and imperfection of the human condition, that Tigerman intentionally replicated. A few years before his death in 2019, he said that, in building the new home for the Co-op, he was trying to create "something that wasn't perfect, that would . . . never be finished."[2] He could well have used these ideas to develop a blueprint for any good bookstore.

Tigerman, who considered architecture an ethical pursuit, joined the Co-op in 1991. He understood that the good bookstore is about interiority. Deep in the browse, many of us move through the space as though we were inside the Mind itself—of the universe or God, depending on one's fancy. And many of us turn inward as we do so, finding the space especially conducive to self-reflection.

• • •

The journalist and Co-op enthusiast Jamie Kalven has suggested that the shape of the bookstore operates as something akin to a literary form.[3] The bookstore offers insight through what the genre-defying writer Mary Cappello calls, in reference to the form of the lecture, "un-pursued apposition,"[4] and "the necessity of getting lost in the shape of one's lostness."[5] What other literary forms might the bookstore resemble?

Perhaps the bookstore is like an encyclopedia, containing all of our knowledge in one place. Or like the *Huainanzi*, a second-century emperor's manual of sorts, a compilation of everything that was known about the way of the world—the celestial bodies, the natural world, time, space, human consciousness, the principles of self-cultivation, characteristics of the sage, and the practicalities of governance. The wise emperor, well read in their *Huainanzi*, would be capable of concentrating on something as small as "the tip of an Autumn hair and something as vast as the totality of space and time."[6]

Perhaps it is like an anthology—a compendium of ideas, tales, mores—a bible for bibliophiles. Or perhaps it better resembles the essay, as Montaigne mastered it, an amble about, considering now this and now that, a wandering series of thoughts that hope to limn a question. Although the essay might literally mean an attempt, implying something unsuccessful, it is the asking, not the answering, that provides the essay its purchase. The essay trucks in many truths, not the achievement of one ultimate truth. Montaigne in his library: "I leaf through now one book, now another, without order and without plan, by disconnected fragments."[7] In the bookstore-as-essay genre, these fragments are the books themselves.

Maybe the bookstore is the commonplace book of the bookseller, who, like the reader compiling their commonplace book, considers a wide range of works and filters in an unquantifiable and unscientific manner, arranging according to the principles of taxonomy that bear a relative internal logic but are by no means definitive or final, ensuring that only the finest—measured on many a scale, but the finest nonetheless—are selected.

Or maybe the bookstore is like the *zuihitsu*—which can be literally translated as "following the brush"—that great pillow-book tradition begun by Sei Shōnagon in the eleventh century that, in the fourteenth century, in Kenkō's hands, reached a form that resembles a bookstore. Kenkō knows that "it wakes you up to take a journey for a while, wherever it might be."[8] In his series of reflections and wanderings, he jots down "at random whatever nonsensical thoughts" enter his head. Not unlike the essay, the *zuihitsu* thrives on rumination, not solutions. "The most precious thing in life," writes Kenkō, "is uncertainty."[9]

Like Tigerman, Kenkō understands that uniformity is undesirable. Leaving something incomplete makes it interesting, he writes,

> and gives one the feeling that there is room for growth. Someone once told me, "Even when building the imperial palace, they always leave one place unfinished." In both Buddhist and Confucian writings of the philosophies of former times, there are also many missing chapters.[10]

If the *zuihitsu* is, as described by a nineteenth-century practitioner of the form, Ishiwara Masaakira, a record of what "one sees and hears, says and ponders, whether frivolous or serious, just as they come to mind," perhaps the literary form that is the space of the bookstore consists of the thoughts that arise in the minds of the browsers—a mélange of references, idle thoughts, the index of personal memories, the poetic lines of others, the ephemera of sensation—and the attention that is diffuse and discursive, but still somehow focused, as these thoughts follow the brush, as it were. Steven Carter, the scholar of Japanese history who translated and edited an anthology of *zuihitsu*, writes that "books pass by like currents in a river, all jumbled together, which is only appropriate since so many books are themselves jumbles of things."[11]

THE ART OF BROWSING IN BOOKSTORES

The good bookstore sells books, but its primary product, if you will, is the browsing experience. Until 1870, when the poet and essayist James Russell Lowell used the word in reference to John Dryden's reading habits, "browse" meant, primarily, to chew cud, to ruminate.

Here, according to the *Oxford English Dictionary*, is one of the earliest written appearances of the word "browse" utilized in this context. "We thus get a glimpse of [Dryden] browsing, he was always a random reader—in his father's library, and painfully culling here and there a spray of his own proper nutriment from among the stubs and thorns of Puritan divinity."[12] And later, Lowell writes of the German polymath G. E. Lessing, "Like most men of great knowledge, as distinguished from mere scholars, he seems to have been always a rather indiscriminate reader, and to have been fond, as Johnson was, of 'browsing' in libraries."[13]

One of the great benefits of the act of browsing is the rumination it evokes. To create a space that is intentional in its gathering of materials meant to provide intellectual and literary stimulation, a space wholly devoted to books, be it a bookstore, a library, or a personal collection, is to understand the fulfillment provided by the activity of rumination and reflection. We are, after all, "of the ruminating kind," John Locke writes of the relationship of thinking to reading, "and it is not enough to cram ourselves with a great load of collections; unless we chew them over again they will not give us strength and nourishment."[14]

To say it more directly, browsing is a form of rumination. Books, like the leaves and shrubs known as the browsage, provide ruminant-readers with their nutrients. What an unparalleled activity it is to browse a bookstore in a state of curiosity and receptivity, chewing one's intellectual cud! The space of a bookstore must be conducive to unhurried rumination, if only to promote good digestion.

We booksellers mark the transformation as our patrons, upon entering the store, leave their everyday concerns at the door, as though stepping into a more thoughtful confine. We know it is our responsibility to create and enclose this space, allowing anyone to enter, but not any *thing*. It's a place for books, just books, and for a certain kind of book whose presence alongside the rest of the collection is meant to create something of a pasture for The Hungry Mind—the name that the erstwhile booksellers gave to their legendary bookstore in St. Paul, Minnesota.

• • •

There are many forms of browsing, and many types of browsers. A non-exhaustive list of those we see in our wilds would include the *flaneur*, who meanders through the stacks, observing, loitering, shuffling; the *sandpiper*, who sees the world in a grain of sand; the *town crier*, who heralds the latest news from the pages of the books on the front table; the *ruminator*, chewing their cud; the *pilgrim*, seeking wisdom, they know not what or where, but knowing that they must find it; the *devotee*, who prays daily, regardless of the season; the *penitent*, who has not lived as they ought and is now seeking redemption, or at least forgiveness; the *palimpsest*, who reads and rereads and knows that every reading leaves its inscrutable mark; the *chef*, who trusts their senses to help them identify the most delectable ingredients; the *initiate*, who doesn't know the mores of the place but is hopeful they might soon belong; the *stargazer*, who takes in the sky with a well-honed attention; the *general*, who sees the stacks as a thing to be conquered; and the *idler*, who just wants to while away the hours among books.

Morley, one of bookselling's greatest champions, laments that most habitués of the bookstore have yet to understand its uses. He knows that bookish spaces are made for the wandering browser, reflecting on sundry matters, as they travel the stacks. He thinks of the bookstore as a great instrument and bemoans the fact that we visit bookstores "chiefly to ask for some definite title," playing the instrument like an amateur. He goes on:

> Aren't we ever going to leave anything to destiny, or to good luck, or to the happy suggestion of some wise bookseller? Too many of our dealings with bookstores remind me, in their innocent ineffectiveness, of children learning to play the piano. I hear their happy ploiterings among the keys, their little tunes and exercises ring in my head in times of softened mood reminding me of all the lovely unfinished melodies of life. But it isn't what a connoisseur would call music.[15]

The *connoisseurs* of the bookshop develop their unique style. They learn divagation. They know to leave a bit of room for inspiration and aspiration.

There are great pleasures awaiting those who submit to this instrument. Samuel Ibn Tibbon, the thirteenth-century Maimonidean, could be describing the browse when he writes, "If your soul be satiate and weary, change from garden to garden, from furrow to furrow, from sight to sight. Then will your desire renew itself and your soul be satisfied with delight." And elsewhere, Ibn Tibbon articulates our position well: "Let your book-cases and your shelves be your gardens and your pleasure-grounds. Pluck the fruit that grows therein, gather the roses, the spices, and the myrrh."[16] He understands the stacks to be a pleasure ground whose verdure remains.

The stroll-about has been a tool for rumination for some time. One of our seminal philosophers even named his school after the up-and-down walk. Aristotle, who was "Plato's most genuine disciple," left Plato's Academy to found his own school. According to Diogenes Laertius's account, Aristotle "made choice of a public walk in the Lyceum where he would walk up and down discussing philosophy with his pupils."[17] I imagine the intellectual descendants of Aristotle, wandering the crooked aisles of the Co-op—modern-day peripatetics—discoursing on the ethical life, heeding the master's wisdom on what makes it all worthwhile: "For without friends no one would choose to live, though he had all other goods."[18]

Epicurus thought the noblest were "most concerned with wisdom and friendship."[19] It was written upon the threshold of his school, known as the garden, "Stranger, here you will do well to tarry. Here our greatest good is pleasure."[20] In 2014, the Seminary Co-op Bookstore adopted this inscription as our guiding principle, imagining no greater aspiration than toward wisdom and friendship, those Epicurean pleasures.

• • •

While a physical location matters, it is the use of that space that creates its culture and its meaning. The basement of the old Seminary Co-op, in the old Chicago Theological Seminary building, entirely unremarkable on its own, became, for so many, a magical labyrinth of books and, perhaps, a sort of literary form. But no longer. It currently houses classrooms for the University of Chicago's Department of Economics and the Becker Friedman Institute for Research in Economics. Just as the cafeteria that once served meals to the seminary students who founded the Seminary Co-op is no longer visible among the scattered bookcases of the current Seminary Co-op, so the old, subterranean Seminary Co-op has left nary a remnant in its original space. The nostalgic and knowing might identify the portal that once led to a most unlikely cave of books, one that was simultaneously cramped and expansive (cramped the aisles; expansive the shelves). Unless the Department of Economics grants them access to the building, however, they will be unable to enter. Even if they gained entry, they would find a spacious, well-lit corridor that bears no resemblance to the crowded labyrinth that inspired generations of readers and is patently unremarkable—not much different from how it would have been found in 1961.

A good bookstore, like a good university, need not necessarily belong to a specific place. If it attracts the literati and the cognoscenti, the curious and the erudite, it will become a space of contemplation and discovery, a shelter for the ruminating kind. We might say, with Bachelard, that "space that has been seized upon by the imagination cannot remain indifferent space subject to the measures and estimates of the surveyor."[21] But the imagination too is portable, and that inestimable element of the bookstore is not stationary.

In his history of reading, Alberto Manguel, an exemplary reader and supremely bookish writer, tells of Abdul Kassem Ismael, the tenth-century grand vizier of Persia, and his 400 camels that carried his collection of 117,000 books when he traveled. Through a dexterous feat of herd indexing, he trained the camels to walk in alphabetical order, lest his collection succumb to the tyrant of chance.[22]

One hundred thousand books were professionally moved from University Avenue to Woodlawn Avenue to fill the new Seminary Co-op's thoughtfully designed bookcases. There might seem something silly about ritual, especially young or visibly constructed rituals, but considering the reputation of the bookstore and what it meant to the community, the enactment of some sort of ritual seemed appropriate. And so, there was a purposeful and symbolic procession of a small selection of books to the new bookstore, carried with a sense of duty and pride by their authors (leaving the alphabetical procession to the professional movers). Here was the philosopher Jonathan Lear moving his *A Case for Irony*, and there was the scholar Kenneth Warren moving his *What Was African American Literature?* The authors acted as priests, leading their congregants to their new temple, sanctifying the space with their talismans, their books. The community now had permission to bring their worship of the life of the mind to the new Seminary Co-op.

The novelist and upstanding literary citizen Aleksandar Hemon delivered the keynote for the Seminary Co-op's grand opening ceremony, during which he both eulogized the old space and identified the cause of the day: the sanctifying of a book space. In his eulogy, he reminded us of

> the low ceiling with heated pipes, no windows, little space—those who reached those depths were willing to endure anything for the kind of high books can produce. Like an opium den, the bookstore was also hard to find. You couldn't just stumble upon it; it was a destination to which your addiction led you. The bookstore was not dimly lit enough for smoking opium, but the layout helped neither air nor customer circulation.[23]

The addiction, as Hemon knew, wasn't merely to reading, or to procuring books, but to the browsing of the stacks. We are pursuing a particular—and mostly wholesome—intoxication provided by these pleasure grounds, this Epicurean garden. And so it seemed, in 2013, that the bookstore was worth not only preserving, but reimagining, and sanctifying.

MAMMON DESCENDS

The cynical observe that Mammon has now descended upon the temple, as a cathedral that once held worship services for seminary students—stained glass intact—now holds seminars for budding economists. Milton Friedman and Gary Becker, after whom the Becker Friedman Institute is named, were both regular patrons and longtime shareholders of the Seminary Co-op. They spent hours browsing the shelves in the basement of that building, one level below the glass cases that now house their Nobel Prizes.

Perhaps the economists can help us create a different model. The economic model of bookstores failed us, not we it. While bookstores are no longer the most efficient or, perhaps, cost-effective method of procuring specific books, the selling of books has always been one of the least interesting services that bookstores provide. The value is, and has always been, at least in the good and serious bookstores, in the experience of being among books—an experience afforded to anyone who enters the space with curiosity and time.

And the yield is discovery, not of what we think we know we want, but of that which we have yet to encounter. While an algorithm might suggest a book that we are likely to enjoy based upon who we've been, or what an advertiser might want us to think we want, nothing can replace the work of browsing to help us discover who we are or who we might become.

The member-owned co-op is built to pay financial dividends to its shareholders. Even if our co-op had been successful in that endeavor—it hadn't been since the early 1990s—it is clear that this sort of structure misses the point. If our goal is to provide cultural value—a dividend of a different sort—and to belong to all who think we might have something to provide them, then our structure should support those ends and our mission state them unequivocally.

In recognition of the limits of our structure, and as we did in developing the old space—grafting a clear vision upon a severely limiting structure—we also took the opportunity presented by the move to build a more deliberate structure. We knew the bookstore must belong to the community, and so its structure should reflect the public good. We knew the product was the space itself—and the browsing grounds created there—and that no retail model would support the maintenance of the very collection that made the store worthy of preservation.* And we knew that the new model should accurately describe our purpose as well as support our mission and our finances in perpetuity.

In 2019, at a meeting presided over by Warren, then president of the board of the Seminary Co-op,

---

* Our beloved collection of Loeb Classical Library titles, for instance, are all sold at a loss, though we charge list price.

the co-op shareholders present voted unanimously to transition the Seminary Co-op from a member-owned cooperative to the first not-for-profit bookstore whose mission is bookselling.

LITTLE FISSURES

There is something of the prospector about the reader lost among books, as there is about the reader lost in a book. Ruskin, speaking of the way of the world, reminds us that writers, scattering bits of wisdom throughout their pages, are just following the method of nature. He describes a phenomenon readers know well: that there is a reticence in the wise whereby one only receives their wisdom as a reward for effort set forth. Likening wisdom to gold, which Ruskin calls "the physical type of wisdom," he sees no reason why the electric forces of the earth don't consolidate gold to an easily accessible spot, from which we might fashion our currency. "But Nature does not manage it so," he writes. "She puts it in little fissures in the earth, nobody knows where: you may dig long and find none; you must dig painfully to find any."[24]

And so it is for the accomplished browser when confronted by a good bookstore. They seek the reward—they hope they are worthy—and they have developed their unique strategy for surveying the crags and fissures, as Ruskin would have it. When we come to a book, he tells us, we must ask ourselves, "Are my pickaxes and shovels in good order, and am I in good trim myself, my sleeves well up to the elbow, and my breath good, and my temper?"[25] And so it must be for the browser, approaching the bookstore, preparing to excavate the gold they seek. "Gold-seekers," Heraclitus says, "dig much earth to find a little gold."[26] But here, as in any work worth doing, the effort is also its own reward.

• • •

Horace Walpole, the English politician and writer, in the first known usage of the word "serendipity," refers to it as *"accidental sagacity,"* by which he means that *"no* discovery of a thing you *are* looking for comes under this description."[27] The scholar Sean Silver, describing serendipity as "the discovery of something useful while on the hunt for something else," has explored the centuries-old appeal of the idea, which clearly predates Walpole's coinage. "If only it could be systematized," Silver imagines the argument unfolding, "induced, lured out of hiding, or otherwise prompted, if the conditions for it could only be prepared, or the mind-set conducive to encountering it could be learned—well, the potential payoffs are immediately obvious."[28] Ruskin might have replied, "But nature does not manage it so."[29]

Perhaps serendipity is not quite as accidental as Walpole made it out to be. In his masterpiece *The Man without Qualities*, the novelist Robert Musil thinks deeply about how to pursue certainty in an uncertain world. Struggling to "achieve a literary representation of a man thinking," he writes:

> When someone asked a great scientist how he managed to come up with so much that was new, he replied: "Because I never stop thinking about it." And it is surely safe to say that unexpected insights turn up for no other reason than that they are expected.[30]

In other words, seemingly accidental phenomena are often quite deliberate.

The wise readers have a talent for finding the right book at the right time—they are masterful prospectors and know that wisdom rarely bestows unearned rewards. On some level, discoveries occur because we are searching. It's that simple. If serendipity is the discovery of something useful while on the hunt for something else, the expert browser doesn't even bother with the conceit that there need be a something else for which to hunt.

To the *idler*, as to the *flaneur*, the stroll is an end in itself. There is a curiosity about what might come next, a receptivity to whatever might arise, and a conviction that whatever it is, it will be of interest. The *idler* gazes upon the physiognomy of the stacks and needs no further stimulation to pass the hours in pleasant reverie.

The *pilgrim* restlessly seeks what they do not know. Again, there can be something of the quest in the reader finding their way among books. There is an urgency in the search and a sense—a conviction, perhaps—that around the corner, in the next nook, will be *the* book that will arise to meet this moment. For now, that bookish prospector passes the hour in deep attention.

In most of these cases, the work of the bookseller, creating just the right conditions, is silent. There is a certain style of bookselling that prides itself on its invisibility.

• • •

There are forms of idleness that energize as there are forms of productivity that are wasteful. Some bookstores have created phone-free zones, acknowledging that we spend much of our day browsing ephemera in search of nothing worthwhile, consumed by the pull of the vacuous, and that the bookstore might represent an opportunity to focus on something more meaningful. Good bookstores create an environment that is its own argument against digital distraction and a reminder of what stimulation and fulfillment meandering attention can yield. While the scroll through one's phone might resemble a browse, the higher-quality browsage in a bookstore reveals the quickly fading verdure of our manic and distracted age, loosening its pull without stricture.

Rumination focuses and diffuses the attention simultaneously. This sort of thinking takes one out of oneself so as to be returned to oneself; it is a means and an end. It is ephemeral, and it yields enduring pleasures. It is a habit of mind that gives both reason and intuition, both focus and idleness, both engagement and detachment, their due. Rumination allows us to skim the surface of known depths and take a periodic plunge.

We move through, and are perpetually immersed in, landscapes that hold the networks of relations through which we develop an understanding of ourselves and others, and of our collective place in the world. The perpetual unfolding of this world of perception against which we measure ourselves is what we mean when we consider our landscapes. The novelist Marilynne Robinson writes that the great service a community performs for its members is giving a sense of the possible; closing off that sense of the possible is the great disservice the ungenerous community performs.[31] For those who know how to use them, book spaces are a model of the generosity that a community might offer its citizens.

ADJACENCIES

What the French novelist Georges Perec describes as the twofold problem of a library is also the twofold problem of a bookstore: "A problem of space first of all, then a problem of order." Perec is clear that he is not referring to "a small-minded temptation towards an individual bureaucracy: one thing for each place and for each place its one thing."[32] He wants to allow for the serendipitous discovery.

We hope our browsers will be stimulated, sur-
prised, and only a bit confused by the taxonomies
and arrangements. Tigerman created the interior
structure, but the booksellers create the classifications of the Seminary Co-op. There is a wise ambiguity in the architecture of the sections, as there is in
the organization of the shelves themselves, evocative
as Wallace Stevens's ideal poem, which, he tells us,
"must resist the intelligence almost successfully."[33]

A bookseller's taxonomies tend to be among the
unique components of their store's identity. How a
bookseller orders their collection dictates the logic
and serendipities of the browse. Manguel tells us that
the Sumerians called catalogers "ordainers of the
universe."[34] Wendy Doniger, the pioneering Indologist
and a Co-op member since 1978, viewed Cella as just
such an ordainer. Remarking on Cella's shelving of
books on the history of religion in the anthropology
section, Doniger thought that "all our efforts to keep
the two disciplines separate had failed. If Jack saw
that they were the same, they were the same."[35]

• • •

Perec, with a logic and playfulness characteristic of
a great Oulipian, explored the art of arranging one's
books.*

* To give a sense of his commitment, number three on Perec's list
of "Some of the Things I Really Must Do Before I Die" was "arrange
my bookshelves once and for all."

Like the librarians of Babel in Borges's story, who are looking for the book that will provide them with the key to all the others, we oscillate between the illusion of perfection and the vertigo of the unattainable. In the name of completeness, we would like to believe that a unique order exists that would enable us to accede to knowledge all in one go; in the name of the unattainable, we would like to think that order and disorder are in fact the same word, denoting pure chance.[36]

Clearly no such unique order exists. There are, however, certain axioms in the art of cataloging:

All classifications are somewhat arbitrary,
despite their internal logic.

Perec lists eleven ways for a reader to arrange their books: ordered alphabetically by continent or country, color, date of acquisition, date of publication, format, genre, major periods of literary history, language, priority for future reading, binding, and series.[37]

I have known readers who organize their books by the author's birth year, date read, publisher, size, geography, or, of course, the classic method: alphabetical by author. Jonathan Swift organized his library in order to impress his visitors, expecting them to read the collection the way they might read a book.[38]

All classifications result in evocative adjacencies.

Alphabetization exists to help locate specific books. However it is imagined, the bookstore must ensure that the utilitarian can locate their specific book with ease while it still serves the needs of the serendipitous browser. Nevertheless, the layout is designed for those who want to be so encompassed by books as to feel swaddled in them. Or perhaps cradled in them, like Osaragi Jirō's bed for his books, which is surrounded by bookshelves "at head and foot and then close on both sides." As he writes in his *zuihitsu*, "The shelves are so full of books that I have only to stretch out my hand and it will fall on something I like." And while he acknowledges the "innocent pleasure it is to experience the delight of nodding off while reading a difficult book," clearly using the bed to both read and nap, he has lost any sense of whether the bed is there for him or for the books.[39]

The reader skims the spines of the volumes whose adjacencies seem no less coincidental by virtue of their alphabetical arrangement. Toni Morrison, Bharati Mukherjee, Alice Munro, Haruki Murakami, Iris Murdoch, Albert Murray, Robert Musil, Vladimir Nabokov, and R. K. Narayan are unlikely neighbors, and the patron of a good bookstore will find a good selection of the works of each nestled in a bookcase.

While we have alphabetizations in given sections, there are endless refinements one might make. A philosophy section, for instance, might include the full range of the discipline, including popular titles, specialist titles, technical volumes, and primary and secondary literature. Or the categories might be more specific, helping the lover of wisdom make their way through epistemology, logic, ethics, metaphysics, or aesthetics, considering the branches of philosophy discretely. Or they might consider organizing by certain schools of thought: Platonism, Cynicism, Epicureanism, Stoicism, Empiricism, Idealism, Humanism, Pragmatism, and Existentialism, say.

I like to imagine a bookstore's philosophy collection classified by sections named for other books. For instance, we might create a system based on lost Aristotelian treatises. Sections like "Exhortation to Philosophy," "On Being or Having Been Affected," "On Controversial Questions," "Solutions of Controversial Questions," "On the Idea," "Of the Desirable and the Contingent," "Analogies," "Propositions," "Controversial Propositions," and "Laws of the Mess-Table" might provide unpursued appositions that would delight the modern-day peripatetic.[40]

Universal classification is impossible.

The bookseller is not bound by classifications defined by academic disciplines, the Dewey Decimal System, Book Industry Standards and Communications (BISAC) codes, or the Library of Congress, but we do use them to inform assemblages that help readers find books. That is the sole purpose of the taxonomy. There is no grander statement about the types and terrains of knowledge. And so a smart, intimate store like Phinney Books in Seattle maintains just two sections: "Made-up" and "True"—categories that authors like Claudia Rankine, Eliot Weinberger, Valeria Luiselli, and many more would defy.

City Lights Booksellers maintains sections like "Topographies and Somalogistics," "Evidence," "Radical Black Imagination," "Belles-Lettres," "Stolen Continents," and "Muckraking." McNally Jackson's commitment to categorizing literature by geographical regions is even more specific than City Lights Booksellers' approach, from whom they gleaned the inspiration. They have also utilized categories like "Phenomena," "Of the Moment," "Escapes," and "How to Be in the World." The booksellers can be trusted to build collections that stimulate an inspired browse, even if the categories seem odd at first glance.

Perhaps a bookstore might build a system based on Weinberger's list of excellent book titles, "Bibliography (The Cloud Bookcase)." They would include sections like "Arcane Notes on the Cultivation of True Nature," "Biographies of Presumed Immortals," "Comprehensive Collection of True Facts Concerning the Land of Bliss," "Essay on the Depths of the Mind in the Great Void," "Essentials for Preserving Life," "Hymns to the Five Planets," "Marvelous Stanzas for Resuscitating Corpses," "Notes to Be Kept Inside a Pillow," "Poems Made While Beating the Ground," "Questions of Mystery at Times of Serenity," and "Treatise on the Art of Sitting and Forgetting."[41] While I don't imagine we would think of them in quite the same way, my bookselling kin would undoubtedly have bountiful selections for each of these sections.

All collections, upon reclassification, create new, felicitous pairings.

Good bookselling requires a constant reevaluation of the adjacencies created by our cataloging principles. The legendary bookseller Paul Yamazaki, who has spent over five decades at the sublime City Lights Booksellers, one of our finest bookstores, said that "a bookstore is somewhat like an ocean—it may look the same, but it is always changing, if you are a careful observer."[42]

In 2015, we created a comparative religion section and a Hinduism section, leaving the anthropology and South Asian history sections, respectively, just a bit more focused. William James, Mircea Eliade, and Karen Armstrong were in each other's company, and our world religions wing, adjacent to anthropology and philosophy, now contained one of the oldest and richest faiths. Professor Doniger's students now had their proper browsage.

No collections are final.

As Borges wrote, "nothing is built on stone, everything on sand, but our duty is to build as if sand were stone."[43] Though the ground beneath us will shift, we present our current taxonomy in the spirit of a proposition, arguing only that this grouping will create interesting grounds of discovery. We, of course, know, as Manguel notes, that "every library is a library of preferences, and every chosen category implies an exclusion."[44] Our work is to select and assemble, making the discordant wilds of bookish inquiry manageable.

We booksellers hope to approximate an order and create pleasurable browsage. These are clearly complementary impulses. But we also know, as Manguel points out, that "whatever classifications have been chosen, every library tyrannizes the act of reading, and forces the reader—the curious reader, the alert reader—to *rescue* the book from the category to which it has been condemned."[45] All books are perceived, initially, according to their place in the constellation of books, until they are engaged apart from the others; they will only be discovered, however, in relation to others.

THE INFINITE EXPANSE OF HUMAN THINKING IN ONE PLACE

For so many of us, the landscape of books is often enough, and we don't know that we are seeking anything beyond the bookish space itself. This was clear to Tigerman, who said that "what was needed was the presence of books everywhere." To accomplish this, he established "a series of 'figural voids' polygonally disposed to each other that would behave as a kind of maze. 'Windows' in these figural voids would act as a 'beckoning fair one,' enticing the customer into the next space."[46]

Alena Jones, manager of the Seminary Co-op, and one of the booksellers whose soul incarnate in the bookshop Lear imagined in his help-wanted ad, considers the figural voids of the artist James Turrell's Skyspaces, in light of the filtration and organization of the bookseller. Turrell frames a specific section of sky and invites the viewer to sit beneath it. Jones writes:

> It slices up or apportions something infinite and sets it in front of us on a totally different scale. Yet this doesn't limit or bind the sky's infinite or profound qualities—it allows us to see them heightened in a smaller space, allows us a human-scaled entry point when before the expanse had been overwhelming.[47]

By framing the vast, open space, the Skyspace help us make connections, refine our vision, and deepen our engagement. "Bookstores do a similar thing," Jones observes, "by bringing together the infinite expanse of human thinking into one space." In this space,

> you have access to something sublime that completely subsumes your meager human frame. You become part of this bounded space that is crack-

ling with new connections. Things that are utterly mundane to you are charged with creativity and meaning by their proximity to things that have truly moved you. You become an essential node in making these connections, in watching the dense fabric emerge from what you had previously understood to be just a monochrome plane of thought. The longer you spend in the store, the more complex, the more varied, and the more unified the expanse becomes. Searching longer doesn't exhaust the store of ideas, just as gazing longer up into a Skyspace doesn't ever result in you fully seeing or understanding the sky. It just continuously unfolds in front of you; the processes of framing this space specifically and then gazing into it initiate the act of unfolding.[48]

Jones and her bookselling kin create their frames and invite the *stargazers* to identify their asterisms within these constellations of books.

THIN AND THICK PLACES

Upon summiting Croagh Patrick, Gregory Schenden, the Catholic chaplain at Georgetown University, spoke of the feeling of transcendence he had as he beheld the islands of Clew Bay in the distance. His friend Fergus told him about the Celtic concept of thin places, "those physical places where earth seems to draw closer to heaven." Schenden, in an attempt to understand what made a site "thin," acknowledged that the original Celtic notion allows for religious and secular locales "where we find ourselves amid something far greater and, in doing so, we become our more authentic selves." He names two of the country's oldest and most committed serious bookstores, the Seminary Co-op and City Lights, as two thin places where one can "get lost among the stacks of such bookstores, where time fades away into something far greater."[49]

I have experienced these bookstores in just the same way. Whether making my A-to-Z way through the poetry room at City Lights Booksellers in San Francisco, finding a new literary nonfiction subsection in the basement of Strand Books in New York City, meandering through the vast philosophy and religion sections on the third floor of Moe's Books in Berkeley, or taking in the entirety of the collection at Source Booksellers* in Detroit in one delightful gulp, there is no doubt that, in these stores, I am drawn closer to some sort of heaven.

But if there are thin places, then certainly that must mean that there are also thick places. Thoreau

* Many of our best booksellers were raised in bookstores. The current owners of Strand Books and Powell's Books are third-generation owners. Moe's Books, founded by Moe and Barbara Moskowitz, is currently owned and operated by their daughter, Doris Moskowitz. Sarah McNally, who founded McNally Jackson, is the daughter of Holly and Paul McNally, who founded the Canadian bookselling chain McNally Robinson. Janet Webster Jones, the inimitable and inspired founder of Source Booksellers, currently runs the shop with her daughter, Alyson Turner.

writes of a certain sort of thickness that is detrimental to our sense of benevolence and, perhaps, godliness. "We meet at the post-office," he writes, "and at the sociable, and about the fireside every night; we live thick and are in each other's way, and stumble over one another, and I think that we thus lose some respect for one another."[50]

Perhaps the good bookstore then is a thin place that occasionally resembles a thick place—after all, it is abundant with people, ideas, and books. Thick though it might appear, we don't lose respect for one another, as Thoreau would have it. We might be in each other's way here and there, as we face the infinite expanse of human thought in one place, but that is different from living thick, seeing as this sort of encounter with others is conducive to the creation of, as the novelist and pacifist Nicholson Baker called the Seminary Co-op, "a peaceable kingdom of books."[51]

CHAPTER TWO
Abundance

The world is a great Volume and man the Index of that Booke.

—JOHN DONNE, "Sermon Preached at the Funeral of
Sir William Cokayne," *The Sermons of John Donne*, 189

THE LAWS

In 1931, the mathematician S. R. Ranganathan, after spending eight years as the university librarian at Madras, articulated one of the most influential attempts at establishing principles for book guardianship. Coining the term "library science," Ranganathan proposed the following "Five Laws of Library Science":

1. Books are for use.
2. Every reader his or her book.
3. Every book its reader.
4. Save the time of the reader.
5. The library is a growing organism.[1]

With minimal adaptation, the Five Laws of Library Science are directly applicable to the art of bookselling. We have already discussed the importance of reading ornate volumes—books are for use. In chapter 5, I will posit that booksellers should *respect* the time of the reader, which would include the saving of it, but also a certain expenditure of it. In this chapter, we will think through the other three laws as we consider abundance in publishing, books, bookstores, and ourselves.

I would like to add a sixth law, "Warburg's Law of the Good Neighbor," established by Aby Warburg, the scion of a wealthy German family and founder of the Library for Cultural Studies. "According to Warburg,"* Manguel explains, "the book with which one was familiar was not, in most cases, the book one needed. It was the unknown neighbor on the same shelf that contained the vital image."[2] If we are to understand the art of bookselling and the practice of the bookseller, we must first understand the discernment and arrangement required in crafting a good bookstore.

The novelist Italo Calvino thinks that books are written so that they might "take [their] place on a hypothetical bookshelf." Their presence "alters the shelf."[3] Thoughtful booksellers understand this intuitively. They think in shelves, cases, sections, and stores, deliberately creating the conditions that reveal the truth of Warburg's Law and the Five Laws of Library Science.

• • •

* Warburg's sister-in-law was a Loeb. Her brother James founded the Loeb Classical Library, an extensive collection of which has long been a marker of many a good bookstore.

Before we continue, I should note a few differences between libraries and bookstores, as it might seem as though our public libraries provide all the virtues of the bookstore. While it is certainly true that the ideal of a library—a landscape abundant with books, open to all, tended by book professionals (readers of reading)—is very similar to the aspirations of the good bookstore as a grounds for ruminative browsing, there are nonetheless meaningful differences between them that emphasize the particular relationship that bookstores cultivate between book and reader.

In their ideal forms, libraries do not replace bookstores but rather make a great complement to them. The collection of a bookstore, generally mostly intact, is a more reliable expression than the always incomplete library collection. If the librarians do their jobs well, a considerable portion of the collection will be dispersed among the community at any given time. If the booksellers do their job well, books purchased by customers are restocked swiftly, and the intended collection is restored for the browser.

There are virtues to book ownership as there are to communal collections, though the virtues are quite different. A patron who borrows a book is beholden to a calendar that privileges quick reads—books that both read quickly and want to be read soon. How many books must ripen on our shelves before we are ready for them? And how too might we properly digest a lush, elusive, or powerful book without marking and annotating it, and without having it at hand that we might reread bits and pieces? A certain intimacy is lost when the book is unowned.

On a more dispiriting note, many of our libraries have evolved over time, moving away from their former mission of being a communal repository of books and toward something more like a general community center. This is clear from the evolution of the Five Laws of Library Science, which have been adapted for our current library and information scientists. Different versions of the laws proposed between 2004 and 2019 account for media, websites, social media, and knowledge more generally. While municipalities offering services to their communities, such as internet access, civic activities, maker labs, and tool-lending libraries, is a wonderful development, there is no reason why these services should be adjuncts to the library when they would fit more naturally in a community center. As it stands, these services, currently offered by many libraries, dilute the original purpose of a library as a storehouse of books, just as socks and tchotchkes dilute the bookstore's ability to do the same.

Libraries are treasures, of course, and the idea of the public library is revolutionary. It is difficult to imagine, in a world without public libraries, a contemporary introducing the concept and effectively convincing the general public, or even philanthropists, to finance it. As we explore models that might support the good bookstore, let's celebrate the revolutionary fact of the establishment of a public library model in the nineteenth century.

• • •

That we might understand just how overwhelming the abundance of a bookish space can be for the civilian, all professional keepers of book palaces should consider as required reading chapter 100 of Musil's *The Man without Qualities*, entitled "General Stumm invades the State Library and learns about the world of books, the librarians guarding it, and intellectual order."[4] Stumm, in search of "the greatest idea in the world," can also help us illustrate something familiar to many of us when we are searching the abundant stacks for *the* book whose enchantment will reveal, or return us to, our paradise.

Stumm is both *pilgrim* and *initiate*, searching for the key to it all, but with tremendous ignorance of the tools available to him; a soldier, he reverts to the only strategies he knows. He faces the abundance of the library with rapacity before sensing that his militaristic approach might serve him poorly in this endeavor. Likening the rows of books to "a garrison on parade," Stumm has "penetrated the enemy's lines."

> I felt nailed to the spot—the whole world seemed to be one enormous practical joke! And I'm telling you, even though I'm feeling a bit calmer about it, there's something radically wrong somewhere![5]

He goes on to make an argument that is off-putting in its downright unbookish carnage, but compelling nonetheless. "You may say it isn't necessary to read every last book," he tells our librarian; unable to relieve himself of military metaphors, he continues, "Well it's also true that in war you don't have to kill every last soldier, but we still need every one of them. You may say to me that every book is needed too."[6] The Talmudic sage Tanhuma thought similarly about a gentler matter, the words of the Torah, teaching, "All words of Torah need one another, for what one word closes, another opens."[7]

Good bookstores reflect a Whitmanian sense of self: they contain multitudes. They contain familiar titles and as yet undiscovered volumes. Like our personal libraries and canons, they are aspirational, containing books that reflect who we think we are, as well as books that help us develop in new directions. There are some books, we know, whose proximity will provide us with pleasure, even if they remain unread.* We can understand why Morley felt assured "that no one ever entered a bookstore without having in his soul some fertilizable granule of human possibility."[8]

Yes, every reader "his or her book," but no store is for every reader. A good bookstore must develop its filters and selections, and thus its character. If done well, the seams between the bookstore and its community will be invisible; if done superbly, the community

---

* Walter Benjamin (*Illuminations*, 62) tells of Anatole France's rejoinder to a "philistine" who, after admiring France's library, asked Monsieur France if he had read all of the books. "Not one-tenth of them," France replied. "I don't suppose you use your Sèvres china every day?"

wouldn't imagine its life without the store, so seam-lessly does the bookstore bind that community.

The Seminary Co-op established itself as a schol-arly store built for the serious general reader as much as for the scholar. E. M. Forster, in his appreciation of the London Library, describes it as "pay[ing] a hom-age to seriousness and to good sense." He might well have been celebrating the ethos of bookstores like the Seminary Co-op. "It has cherished the things of the mind, it has insisted on including all points of view, and yet it has been selective."[9]

THE ABUNDANCE

There are just *so many* books. What happens when a reader enters a good bookstore? The Seminary Co-op houses nearly 100,000 volumes; what happens when a reader enters a bookstore that houses 20-million-odd pages? If they are attentive, and the filtration of the shopkeeps is of a high quality, they might mark the Jamesian varieties of experience encompassed by the endless, pluralistic tale of human perspectives. And they might understand the famous proclama-tion in Ecclesiastes 12:12, not as a caution, but as a celebration: "Of making many books there is no end."

We connoisseurs know the difference between a storehouse of books and a carefully assembled collec-tion. I have been in stores—Gray Wolf Books in San Leandro and John K. King Books in Detroit come to mind—with well over 100,000 books that could have been culled to a great collection of 50,000 volumes. While I do enjoy the strategizing that is needed for the browse in these sorts of indiscriminate bookstores, navigating the ephemera (outdated technical manuals, books in disrepair, books with their living author's photo on the cover) can be enervating.

In the hands of expert booksellers, however, we become more like Dryden and Lessing, as Lowell describes them: random and indiscriminate readers. We feel like Charles Lamb: "I can read almost anything. I bless my stars for a taste so catholic, so unexcluding."[10] We confess, with Leigh Hunt, "once and for all, that I have a liking for them all. It is my link with the bibliomaniacs, whom I admit into our relationship, because my love is large, and my family pride nothing."[11]

The good bookseller earns their reader's trust. We readers know that the sensibility of the bookseller is discerning, and we know that the good bookseller is a great listener who can identify what we are seeking, even if we are inarticulate in voicing it—and even if we think we don't know what we are seeking.

Of the 28,000 titles the Seminary Co-op sold in 2019, nearly 17,000 were single copies. In other words, each of those 17,000 books was sought by a unique reader. Emerson's "extraordinary *relative* power" of books to intoxicate us and no other is rendered visible by this number. Simply put, book discovery can't be mass-produced; it is a highly individualized endeavor. As Shils points out, it is the availability of many slow-moving lines that makes a good bookshop. This means that, from a purely profit-driven perspective, the good bookstore is bound to stock books it shouldn't. And that a good portion of those 17,000 books would not have been discovered that year if they weren't on our shelves.

THE UNDISCOVERABLE BOTTOM

There are books that are themselves abundant, books for which we go searching in abundant book spaces. Sometimes it is the sensation associated with these private treasures—the books that seem to be written to us alone—that we seek.

Emerson, in a letter to his fellow Transcendentalist Samuel Gray Ward, wrote:

> It happens to us once or twice in a lifetime to be drunk with some book which probably has some extraordinary *relative* power to intoxicate *us* and none other;* and having exhausted that cup of enchantment we go groping in libraries all our years afterwards in the hope of being in paradise again.[12]

Our guides are our curiosity and our intuitive sense that, as Lear said of the Co-op, "around the corner, in the next nook, will be *the* book that unlocks the universe."[13]

---

* The Second Law of Library Science.

The poet and critic Geoffrey O'Brien, in his well-titled book *The Browser's Ecstasy*, longed to discover the book he could not imagine. "The unread book is the life yet to be lived," he reasons, "the promise that there will be new ideas, images never glimpsed. The paradise of futurity is the thousand-page book full of episodes still to come."[14] These enchanting unread books will take different forms.

• • •

While the bookstore itself is abundant, there are books that aspire to their own encyclopedism. Books like Flaubert's *Bouvard and Pécuchet*, Stein's *The Making of Americans*, Joyce's *Ulysses*, and Forrest's *Divine Days* aspire to comprehensive descriptions of knowledge, consciousness, a day, and a week, respectively. *The Man without Qualities* is one of those novels whose capaciousness might yield "the paradise of futurity." In the fifth and final of his six memos for the next millennium, Calvino writes of Musil and the project of literary encyclopedism.* Unlike the noun "encyclopedia," he tells us, "which etymologically implies an attempt to exhaust knowledge of the world by enclosing it in a circle," literary encyclopedism attempts to create something of "an *open* encyclopedia."† These books "are the outcome of a

---

* Literary encyclopedism might certainly serve as one model for Kalven's idea of the bookstore as literary form.

† The Fifth Law of Library Science.

confluence and a clash of a multiplicity of interpre-
tative methods, modes of thought, and styles of expression."[15] Even if they are potential or conjectural,
these works are still striving, despite their uncertainty, toward a sort of totality. Fractured though
they be by the confluence and clash, they still aspire
to a totalizing abundance.

As the French author Pascal Quignard observes,
"Fragments do not exist in nature. The tiniest of
pieces is still the totality."[16] It is written in the *Huainanzi*, "The tip of an autumn hair can get lost in
the unfathomable. This means that what is so small
that nothing can be placed inside it is [the same as]
something so large that nothing can be placed outside of it."[17]

William Blake and Elizabeth Bishop—two poets
with markedly different sensibilities—write of the
sort of sight that sees the world in a grain of sand.
Blake's Isaiah declares that his "senses discover'd
the infinite in everything."[18] Bishop's sandpiper is a
student of Blake's: "Poor bird, he is obsessed!" Told
by the poet, "His beak is focussed," we see him, this
sandpiper, wandering the stacks. "He is preoccupied."
We know the type. "Looking for something, something, something."[19] We too know that we might see
a world in a grain of sand, and so we search the mil-
lions of grains through sheets of interrupting water.

In a book that is both monomaniacal *and* encyclopedic, Melville tells us "foolish mortals" that "Noah's
flood is not yet subsided; two thirds of the fair world
it yet covers."[20] Ahab is hunting Moby-Dick in these

waters, but Ahab is "by nature and long habituation far too wedded to a fiery whaleman's ways, altogether to abandon the collateral prosecution of the voyage." This metaphor might well be as violent as Stumm's, but it gets at something profound. For, Ahab reasons, perhaps correctly in the abstract but clearly absurdly in the concrete, "the more monsters he slew by so much the more he multiplied the chances that each subsequently encountered whale would prove to be the hated one he hunted."[21]

On the first day of the chase, Ahab uses the flight of the herons to finally, at long last, identify Moby-Dick in the depths. At first, Ahab sees only a "white living spot no bigger than a white weasel," but as the whale rises "with wonderful celerity," Ahab marks "two long crooked rows of white, glistening teeth, floating up from the undiscoverable bottom."[22] Melville's ocean is literally unfathomable, which doesn't mean that we can't occasionally behold something that has plumbed the depth and returned with its mute and knowing gestures.

THE GIFTS

Sometimes the *pilgrim* is also an *initiate*, searching not just for the book but also for a key to understanding how to use the bookstore itself. We booksellers become hosts. There are few greater joys than witnessing a reader entering the space for the first time. We know we must be gentle. We know we must provide space for discovery. But just a bit of empathy, as we recall our own first exuberant and overwhelmed engagement with the bookstore, will help.

Methodical and with a naive self-assuredness, Musil's Stumm arrives optimistic that he can accomplish his mission. He has already compiled a list "of all the Commanders in Chief of Ideas," for instance. They have "led sizable battalions of ideas to victory."[23] As it turns out, the military strategy fails him; he is consumed by abundance and defeated by his mathematical calculations. He details his thought process:

> I had been thinking that if I read a book a day, it would naturally be exhausting, but I would be bound to get to the end sometime and then, even if I had to skip a few, I could claim a certain position in the world of the intellect. But what d'you suppose that librarian said to me, as we walked on and on, without an end in sight, and I asked him how many books they had in this crazy library? Three and a half million, he tells me. We had just got to the seven hundred thousands or so, but I kept on doing these figures in my head; I'll spare you the details, but I checked it out later at the office, with pencil and paper: it would take me ten thousand years to carry out my plan.[24]

Let's crunch the numbers. Stumm was generous in his estimation of his own reading prowess. I took to pencil and paper and calculated that reading through the current holdings of the Seminary Co-op would require at least 2,000 years. The state library would take 70,000 years to read through.

Emerson thought it "easy to count the number of pages which a diligent man can read in a day, and the number of years which human life in favorable circumstances allows to reading." And he, like Stumm, was left with a lament, recognizing that even if one were to "read from dawn till dark, for sixty years, he must die in the first alcoves."[25]

I have quantified my own reading life, as it were. While it's true that it is easy to do—a simple enough calculation—I don't know that I recommend it, Stumm and Emerson providing something of a cautionary tale. I smoked cigarettes for twenty years. Once I calculated, conservatively, how many cigarettes I had probably smoked, I was persuaded, at last, that I had smoked my share and promptly quit. I didn't lament for a moment the unsmoked cigarettes.

But once I calculated, liberally, how many books I could read, I grew despondent about all of the acquaintances I would never make. I felt cheated by time and libraries. No matter how many books I could reasonably read, there would be *urgent* books left unread. Those first alcoves are lovely, but what of the second, and the third, and the fourth alcoves?

(If only a book could be read in the time it takes to smoke a cigarette—say, seven minutes—one could get through the full inventory of the Seminary Co-op in a lifetime!)

When I was in my best reading shape, I was reading about 50 books a year, but now I'm grateful to finish half as many. According to the National Center for Health, the average life expectancy of Americans is seventy-six years. Presuming we begin generously, let's say at the age of ten, and proceed generously, assuming a life span of eighty years spent in unremitting reading, lapping 50 books annually, the average American (but above-average reader) will read 3,500 books. The buyers of the Seminary Co-op consider 25,000 new books in a given year, which is no more than 5 percent of the books published annually in the United States. We also consider reordering 25,000 backlist* titles. The iconoclastic writer Gabriel Zaid, whose library contains 10,000 volumes, has noted, "If a person read a book a day, he would be neglecting to read four thousand others, published the same day."[26]

Borges, one of the great readers in history, was appointed director of the National Library of Argentina in 1955, almost simultaneously with his immersion into "the dark world and wide," the blindness passed down to him from his father, grandfather, and great-grandfather, all of whom died blind. Borges's stunning "Poem of the Gifts" begins with a moving affirmation,

---

* Industry definitions vary by publisher and bookseller, but generally, backlist (as opposed to frontlist) books are titles that have been available long enough that publicity campaigns, media attention, and prominent bookstore placement are no longer significant factors in sales. Most books become backlist a year after their release.

Let no one impute to self-pity or censure
The power of the thing I affirm: that God
With magnificent irony has dealt me the gift
Of these books and the dark, with one stroke.

He has lifted these eyes, now made lightless,
To be lords of this city of books[27]

Perhaps the blindness of Borges* makes sense as
a metaphor for the bookish. Of the 900,000 volumes
contained in the National Library of Argentina during Borges's tenure,† even a heroic reader such as he
could only read, at best, 1 percent of the holdings.
Given the discouraging arithmetic quantifying a lifetime of reading, it seems we too are gifted with books
and darkness.

• • •

Let's turn to some eminent librarians for scale.
Charles Coffin Jewett was a couple of years shy of
assuming the position of librarian of the Smithson-
ian Institution when he wrote, in 1846, *The Facts and
Considerations Relative to the Duties on Books*. In his

---

* The blind library director was something of a tradition at the
National Library of Argentina, as José Mármol before him and Paul
Groussac after him were also blind during their tenures. "Long before me," Borges wrote in reference to Mármol, "some other man took
these books and the dark" (Borges, "Poem of the Gifts").

† If, that is, Borges's story "The Book of Sand" takes an accurate
measure.

pamphlet on the matter, he tells us that "the whole number of different volumes published since the invention of the art of printing has been estimated at three million. Of these, one million are German, 800,000 are French, 600,000 English, and only 25,000 American."[28]

One can't help but wonder about the reader the legendary British librarian Lionel McColvin had in mind when he published his short book *How to Use Books*. I imagine the first law of library science, that books are for use, is self-evident to those who would be inclined to read such a volume. Anyone inclined to pick it up was likely to have also figured out already how *they* would like to use books, needing little help from the chief librarian of Westminster. No matter. From it we learn some helpful figures about the state of publishing around the time of the Second World War.

> Before the war 17,000 *different* new books and new editions were published in one year in Great Britain alone, a similar number in Japan, nearly twice as many in pre-Nazi Germany, 7,000 in the United States—and other countries more or less in proportion. The number fell considerably during the war; the total for Great Britain in 1944 was only 6,781. Once conditions become normal again, however, we are likely to exceed the pre-war output because there is considerable accumulation of interesting and important books the publication of which waits only until more labor and material are available.[29]

The accumulation of interesting and important books was clearly considerable, and the labor and materials were ample. According to Zaid,

> Five hundred titles were published in 1550, 2,300 in 1650, 11,000 in 1750, and 50,000 in 1850. In 1550, the cumulative bibliography was approximately 35,000 titles; in 1650 it was 150,000; in 1750 it was 700,000; in 1850 it was 3.3 million; in 1950 it was 16 million; and in 2000 it was 52 million. In the first century of printing (1450–1550), 35,000 titles were published; in the last half-century (1950–2000), there were a thousand times more, 36 million.[30]

These numbers are difficult to fathom, which doesn't necessarily mean they're excessive. After all, "every book its reader." But as one's community is made up of some, not all, readers, the bookseller must sift and select the titles to put on their shelves.

THE GARDEN OF THE MUSES

I go forth in search of books, both for me and for the shop. Publisher catalogs arrive two or three times a year, from dozens of publishers. They are teeming with thousands of books that must find their way into the store and scores of titles that aren't quite right for our community. Thus begins our work—the election, the selection, the *lectio*, as

Nancy described. I think of the British novelist Rose Macaulay who, it turns out, was one of Hemon's opium-eaters, feverishly in search of her bookish high. Macaulay captures the feeling quite well in her delightful essay on bookseller catalogs, collected in *Personal Pleasures*:

> To read these catalogues is like drinking wine in the middle of the morning; it elevates one into that state of felicitous intoxication in which one feels capable of anything. I might control myself and not write to booksellers in haste; there must be a gap between the perusal of the catalogue and my postcard. . . . I will wait until the effects are worn off, and then write a postcard, sober, temperate, moderate, brief, restrained. . . . In short, I am sober again. But I am glad that I was drunk.[31]

And this coming from a reader. Imagine the abject dipsomania of the bookseller upon receiving those catalogs!

• • •

Legend had it that Eldon Speed, the erstwhile director of the Stanford Bookstore, aspired to stock the store with one copy of every book published. Speed was pursuing a twentieth-century vision of an "everything store." The good bookstore's abundant collection, however, is discerning; pruning matters.

Ezra Pound, in his 1934 collection *ABC of Reading,** calls for weeders to help solve the problem of prevalence:

> We live in an age of science and abundance. The care and reverence for books as such, proper to an age when no book was duplicated until someone took the pains to copy it out by hand, is obviously no longer suited to the needs of society, or to the conservation of learning. The weeder is supremely needed if the Garden of the Muses is to persist as a garden.[32]

We must identify professionals whose sensibility in weeding, cultivation, and assemblage can be trusted to build good bookstores. "Meantime the colleges, whilst they provide us with libraries," Emerson tells us, "furnish no professor of books; and I think no chair is so much wanted."[33] While we should celebrate the fact that universities have indeed established occasional professorships of books, focusing on the history of the book as object and cultural artifact, booksellers, those "readers of reading," remain the closest thing we have to Emerson's professor of books.

Like most bookstores, the Seminary Co-op has its front table, which serves as a summary and sampler. Over the years it has become the Front Table,

---

* Seven thousand books were published in America in 1934; it is unclear how many were published in Italy.

a symbol and a concept, in addition to serving as a literal table positioned in the front of the store and stacked with books. It is a landscape worth surveying, with nary a weed to be found. The Front Table features books that most readers won't have seen elsewhere: books from university and academic presses, translations of obscure and not-so-obscure classics, difficult books on the vanguard of a field's scholarship, otherwise underrepresented voices. The Front Table is emblematic of the approach of good bookstores. It reflects a commitment to books that endure and are relevant outside any given publishing season, even if they are featured in their publisher's current catalog.

There are 116 titles stacked on the Front Table. They range across disciplines, but all share the designation of a book that is worthy of, and will repay, close attention. Taken as a whole, they represent an idiosyncratic snapshot of a season's intellectual inquiry, but if we booksellers do our job right, the bulk of the books will endure well beyond the season. Lear, whose books fit comfortably on the Front Table, asked, "What to make of the Front Table?" before attempting an answer. "It is not a secret garden, but it is a garden. Cultivated. Weeded." The Front Table, he tells us, "is not fundamentally about desire or obligation. It is about confrontation."[34]

The Front Table, like the displays throughout the store, provides some relief from the rush of spines in the stacks, creating a rhythm that helps the breathless browser pause. The bookseller's merchandising is thoughtfully composed, like a choreographer's notebook or avant-garde musical score, to support a variety of interpretations in performance. Moving beyond the Front Table, the reader will burrow deep in the stacks and confront the collection. Now the notes accelerate as the reader, facing crowded shelves rich with colorful spines, is interrupted at pleasing but irregular intervals, whether by a book faced out to reveal its cover, as the poor book designer intended, or by the polygonal window that Tigerman designed to populate another field of vision with even more spines, more covers, more beckoning fair ones.

THE INDEX

Borges's protagonist in "The Library of Babel," "like all men of the Library," has "wandered in search of a book, perhaps the catalogue of catalogues."[35] This is the imagined book that my kin use to help the wayward reader return to the path and establish their direction. But that is merely a fantasy. The fact is, expert booksellers have enough of their bookstore's holdings memorized at any given time—they often know, without needing to survey the alphabetical sequence of authors, the precise spot of the book on its shelf—to create a sense of magic and wonder in the reader in search of their book, especially when the reader gives little explicit or accurate information.

One of our booksellers created just such a moment early in my tenure. Jonathan Lear rushed in one morning and, clearly searching for something specific, bypassed the Front Table, which was unlike him. He did not follow his usual route to philosophy or literature but, with some urgency, alighted upon the first couple of cases of poetry. He had merely paused when the bookseller asked if he was looking for the new FSG collection of Yehuda Amichai's poetry. Delighted, and with a tender look of relief, he affirmed that that was *exactly* what he was looking for. "How did you know?" he started to ask, before stopping himself, recognizing the professional bookseller's work he had so hoped that I and my colleagues could carry on.

But sometimes, if the questions are too broad, the reader is beyond help. Stumm's librarian, weakened by Stumm's intensity in his search for the greatest idea in the world, relinquishes the tools of filtration, inviting Stumm to make his own way. Stumm describes the encounter:

> My eyes must have been blazing with such a thirst for knowledge that the fellow suddenly took fright, as if I was about to suck him dry altogether. I went on a little longer about needing a kind of timetable that would enable me to make connections among all kinds of ideas in every direction—at which point he turns so polite it's absolutely unholy, and offers to take me into the catalog room and let me do my own searching, even though it's against the rules, because it's only for the use of the librarians. So I actually found myself inside the holy of holies. It felt like being inside an enormous brain.[36]

At the risk of undermining the project at hand, and my own interest in advocating on behalf of the work of serious bookselling, I will tell you that Stumm could not find "one sensible book to read" in that room. He continues:

> Imagine being totally surrounded by those shelves, full of books in their compartments, ladders all over the place, all those book stands and library tables piled high with catalogs and bibliographies, the concentrate of all knowledge, don't you know, and not one sensible book to read, only books about books. It positively reeked of brain phosphorous, and I felt that I must have really got somewhere. But of course a funny feeling came over me when the man was going to leave me there on my own—I felt both awestruck and uneasy as hell. Up the ladder he scoots, like a monkey, aiming straight at a book from below, fetches it down, and says: "Here it is, General, a bibliography of bibliographies for you"—you know about that? In short, the alphabetical list of alphabetical lists of the titles of all the books and papers of the last five years dealing with ethical problems, exclusive of moral theology and literature, or however he put it, and he tries to slip away.[37]

The work of bookselling, like the work of librarianship, is best practiced by those with a passion for catalogs, for sifting and selecting, for filtering, arranging, and, hopefully, matchmaking. Like O'Brien, we know how "the reader looks at catalogues of titles, watching from his inviolable perch as eras disgorge their novels and treatises and histories, so numerous that in the end what is needed is not a catalogue but a catalogue of catalogues."[38] Like Borges's librarian of Babel, we want to "formulate a general theory of the Library and solve satisfactorily the problem which no conjecture had deciphered: the formless and chaotic nature of almost all the books."[39] If Borges is to be understood clearly here, "formless and chaotic" is also the nature of the elements of the universe.*

THE ARCHIVES OF LONGING

The fourteenth-century Italian poet Petrarch didn't possess his library as much as his library possessed him. "I'm haunted by an inexhaustible passion that up to now I have not managed or wanted to quench. I feel that I have never enough books," he says. "Books delight one in depth, run through our veins, advise us and bind with us in a kind of active and keen familiarity; and an individual book does not insinuate itself alone into our spirit, but leads the way for many more, and thus provokes in us a longing for others."[40]

Books beckon books. Books beget books. And so the reader goes forth in search of books. Good advice

---

* Borges's "The Library of Babel" begins thus: "The universe (which others call the Library). . . ."

abounds. The novelist Doris Lessing, for instance, thinks that "there is only one way to read, which is to browse in libraries and bookshops, picking up books that attract you, reading only those, dropping them when they bore you."[41] Virginia Woolf, whose father, Leslie Stephen, served as president of the London Library, thinks that the only advice one reader can give another "is to take no advice, to follow your own instincts, to use your own reason, to come to your own conclusions." We would do well to embrace her advice on the art of browsing:

> To admit authorities, however heavily furred and gowned, into our libraries and let them tell us how to read, what to read, what value to place upon what we read, is to destroy the spirit of freedom which is the breath of those sanctuaries. Everywhere else we may be bound by laws and conventions—there we have none.[42]

And so we build our personal canons. Mine consists of fifty or so authors whose works I find myself returning to, whose oeuvres I long to read entire and then reread. It is the Nobel Laureate Elias Canetti—he brings up the rear of my canon—who tells us that "true spiritual life consists in *rereading*."[43]

Calvino, in considering the importance of "books of all time," urges the reader to invent their own "ideal library of classics" composed "half of books we have read and that have really counted for us, and half of books we propose to read and will presume will come to count—leaving a section of empty shelves for surprises and occasional discoveries."[44] José Gaos, Ortega y Gasset's student, said that "every private library is a reading plan."[45] Susan Sontag, another Seminary Co-op member, called her library an archive of longings.[46]

I sometimes imagine an open-air market, like the bookstalls on College Street in Kolkata, where, instead of selling textbooks, we passionate and enthusiastic booksellers stock only our personal canons at our stalls, hoping we might supply the "surprises and occasional discoveries" with which the reader might fill those empty shelves. What a wonderful browse that would be! A street filled with heartily endorsed books, as though the "electric forces of the earth" did in fact carry all of the gold to the mountaintop.

But, of course, these stalls should be subject to Lessing's and Woolf's good advice. After all, no book suits all palates, and no canon—in cultures that have done away with furred and gowned authorities at any rate—is shared between more than a few. This is a fact worthy of celebration. Our culture, as Zaid writes, "is a conversation without a center":

The true universal culture isn't the utopian Global Village, gathered around a microphone; it is the Babel-like multitude of villages, each the center of the world. The universality accessible to us is the finite, limited, concrete universality of diverse and disparate conversations.[47]

So our canons belong to us alone, but our bookstores are created by and reflective of our communities. "Books," Hemon tells us, "are manuals for being in the world."[48] They are critical materials in the construction of the self, in the building of a good life. May we all build our bookstalls, or our book-beds, that we might better build ourselves. "Who are we," Calvino asks, "who is each one of us, if not a combinatoria of experiences, information, books we have read, things imagined? Each life is an encyclopedia."[49] And a community is expressed in its good bookstore.

CHAPTER THREE
Value

The light of the sun is far different than the light of the lamps.
—CICERO, "Pro Caelio," in *Orations*, 491

THE PRICE OF A SMALL BOX OF CIGARETTES

Richard de Bury amassed the largest private library in England in his time, which was the time of Dante and Petrarch (with whom he corresponded), and the time before Gutenberg—a time when every book was unique. De Bury's exuberance about books has something of the bookseller's professional passion. He speaks of authors "whose praises the longest chapter would not suffice to declare," and he warns that "those things are not to be reckoned small without which great things can't exist."[1] Things, perhaps, like the bookstore.

Nearly seven hundred years after he first published his *Philobiblon*, de Bury can help us establish the question at the core of the conundrum of bookselling: How might we build a model for bookstores? In a chapter entitled "How in Buying Books the Price Is to Be Fixed," de Bury asks, "If it is wisdom alone that makes the price of books (and wisdom is an infinite treasure for man), and if the value of books is unspeakable (as our premises suppose), how shall the bargain be proved dear when the good that is purchased is infinite?" How indeed? After all, de Bury tells us, books "are the treasured wealth of the world, the fit inheritance of generations and nations, necessities of life."[2] No exploration of the value of bookstores can begin without considering the value of books themselves.

Good bookstores are a repository for great books and a testing ground for recently published aspirants to greatness. The bookseller helps create the canons of the future, if only by selecting certain titles for the perennial collection, ensuring that, in a corollary to Warburg's Law of the Good Neighbor, a book's status is elevated by its proximity to books of the ages. Or to put it another way, a book becomes great when it is not out of place among books of the ages.

Bessarione, the fifteenth-century cardinal, spoke reverently of the sorts of books that today sell slowly and unprofitably, but whose import is profound. He remarked on the wisdom they transmit, and their dignity, majesty, and sanctity. These books "live, they converse, they talk to us, they teach, guide, and console us, and bring near the most remote things, putting them before our eyes."[3] We should as soon place a monetary value on the work of the cultivation of the soul as we do on the work of cultivating our contemporary canons: the process is immeasurable.

What the English essayist Thomas Carlyle said about the good of the book is quite applicable to the bookstore: it "is not the facts that can be got out of it, but the kind of resonance that it awakes in our own minds." And we entirely agree when he tells us that a book "may strike out a thousand things, may make us know a thousand things which it does not know itself."[4] We are also reminded that the rules of standard commerce are ill equipped to support our industry.

• • •

Value increases with scarcity. But scarcity can also result from our undervaluing something of great value. We might consider it thus: there is an inflated value based on scarcity and a scarcity based on deflated value. While the things that are deemed of value for no other reason than their scarcity grow more valuable by dint of increasing scarcity, those things that are scarce by dint of being undervalued are likely to pass into extinction.

Bookstores are scarce because we undervalue them, and good bookstores are scarce because we undervalue our cultural wealth. Our only model of bookselling, inherited from traditional retail, overvalues efficiency and neglects a wise inefficiency, a nurturing of what the Japanese scholar Okakura Kakuzō called, in his magisterial *The Book of Tea*, "the subtle use of the useless."[5]

"Every great bookstore allows the reader to get lost in it," Hemon tells us, reflecting on the Seminary Co-op specifically. How do we put a price on the browsing experience, which is also the experience of immersion in a physical space devoted to books?

Hemon continues: "Walking into a bookstore means plunging into a discombobulating field of endless possibilities. A great bookstore is a total environment, a space where nothing except books seems to exist fully, where everything else is either not important or already in the books."[6]

Clearly bookstores are of tremendous value, and not by virtue of their scarcity, scarce though they may be. Their scarcity is a result of our mismeasurement of their value. How do we measure the value of these immersive bookish environments? How do we finance the cost of building these gardens and pleasure grounds? How, for that matter, do we evaluate the worth of the books themselves? Quite irrationally, it turns out—that is, in a way completely incommensurate with their worth. McColvin writes, "Thousands of interesting and well-produced books may be purchased for the price of a seat at the cinema or a small box of cigarettes, and if only readers appreciated the lasting pleasure of well-chosen books they would regard them as by far the better investment for their money."[7] The average consumer who would think nothing of spending $17 on a couple of packs of cigarettes, or a couple of lattes and some baked goods, bristles at spending the same amount for a copy of a book that might provide untold hours of reflection and unquantifiable fulfillment.

I don't continue to derive pleasure from—nor even recall—what I had for breakfast last week, much less last year, but I can tell you what I was reading when I took my first bookselling job in 1994: *Tell Me How*

Long the Train's Been Gone by James Baldwin. The list price of the 1969 mass-market paperback edition, which my mother bought soon after it was published, was $1.25. In 1994, when I read her copy, the value would have been $5.23—or about the price of grabbing a couple of slices of pizza with a friend. As it turns out, Baldwin's novel now costs $17, which, had I purchased it in 1994 for $17, would have been as valuable a $17 expenditure as I made that year. And come to think of it, the book still beckons me from my bookshelf, offering memories and evoking the affective quality of the period in which I read it.

We are trained to look for bargains, and companies like Amazon, cynically at best, destructively at worst, have helped us further devalue books and the tremendous amount of thoughtful and difficult work that goes into creating them, publishing them, and selling them. *Tell Me How Long the Train's Been Gone* is currently discounted 23 percent on the Amazon website. This sort of price reduction signals that at $13 the book is worth what, at $17, is a bad deal for the rational consumer. But certainly, the rationality of homo economicus applies to evaluation, not merely savings; in order to identify a bargain, we must develop skills as assessors.

• • •

I have great respect for the discipline of political economy. I have not studied it deeply, and so I write with caution when discussing its history and its systemic solutions. But perhaps there is room for a layperson's reflections. After all, I am not entirely lacking in qualifications.

As a homo economicus, I have wondered how we can possibly use the same currency for basic needs, luxuries, and that which yields profound fulfilment. I have also been able to answer with a confident "nay!" the question posed by the Renaissance scholar Nuccio Ordine:

> Are debts contracted with the banks and high finance powerful enough to wipe the slate clean at a stroke and cancel the most *important* debts that, over the centuries, we have contracted with those who made us the gift of an extraordinary artistic and literary, musical and philosophical, scientific and architectural heritage?[8]

As a homo civicus, I have longed for the ancient politicians who "talked incessantly about customs and virtues," as Jean-Jacques Rousseau describes them, rather than ours, who "talk only about trade and money."[9] And, with Victor Hugo, I have been embarrassed by our legislative bodies' miserly allocation of funds toward intellectual and artistic endeavors. I too imagine the proportional sums "of a private individual, with an income of one thousand five hundred francs, who annually set aside for his own intellectual culture . . . the absolutely modest sum of five francs and who, on a day of renewal, decided to save five centimes of his own culture."[10]

As a reader, I have identified with the poet Théophile Gautier, who honored the "cobbler's illustrious trade"; nevertheless, he and I would "rather have a shoe whose upper has come away than a poorly rhymed verse, and . . . I would willingly do without boots rather than poetry."[11] With George Gissing's alter ego Henry Ryecroft, I too, as hungry for literature as for food, have "paced the pavement . . . coppers in my pocket, eyeing the stall: two appetites within me." Ryecroft makes his choice: "The book was bought, and as he made shift with a dinner of bread and butter he gloated over the pages."[12] I completely understand.

As an author, I have understood Ernest Renan's reluctance to accept money for the sale of the book, as I too can't see "any common measure between the expression of thoughts . . . and the coin of the realm."[13]

As a lifelong bookseller, I have thought, with St. Jerome, that "it is not for the same man to ascertain the value of gold coins and of writings," and, with Quignard, that "art is among the oldest prehuman practices and is much older than money, into which nothing from the sphere of art can be converted."[14] And yet, I have practiced exchange, liquidated excess inventory,* and quantified goods, price, profits, and losses.

---

* Any bookseller can tell you about how horrified they were when they first learned that, in order to get credit from publishers, they were required to tear the covers off of books and destroy the remaining pages.

I know I can't offer systemic solutions—so many better minds have tried—but perhaps I can limn the problem and consider some models that might help serious bookselling persist.

COMMODITY AND GIFT

Lewis Hyde, in his influential book *The Gift*, explores the difference between the gift and the commodity, between value and worth: "A commodity has value and a gift does not. A gift has worth." He defines value as "the comparison of one thing with another," while defining worth as a reference to "those things we prize and yet say 'you can't put a price on it.'"[15] As the qualities that we prize the most are not transferable—as Musil says of love, introspection, and humility, and Whitman says of wisdom, which, he tells us, "cannot be pass'd from one having it to another not having it"[16]—they have no exchange value, which doesn't mean that they are worthless, only, as the vintage credit card commercial will tell you quite cynically yet quite accurately, "priceless." Hyde formulates it thus:

> Even if we have paid a fee at the door of the museum or concert hall, when we are touched by a work of art something comes to us which has nothing to do with the price. . . . The spirit of an artist's gifts can wake our own. The work appeals, as Joseph Conrad says, to a part of our being which is itself a gift and not an acquisition.[17]

If we are to deliberately build a structure to support good bookstores, we must acknowledge the economy of the gift alongside the economy of the commodity.

• • •

Renowned as a pioneering art critic, Ruskin thought his book on "the first principles of Political Economy," *Unto This Last*, his best, "that is to say, the truest, rightest-worded, and most serviceable."[18] Mohandas Gandhi thought it was one of the two most captivating books by a contemporary (the other was Tolstoy's *The Kingdom of God Is Within You*).[19] Under its "magic spell," he discovered some of his "deepest convictions," the ideals of dignity, simplicity, and community.[20]

Ruskin considers what he calls the five great intellectual professions: the soldier, the pastor, the physician, the lawyer, and the merchant. About the merchant, he says,

Observe, the merchant's function . . . is to provide for the nation. It is no more his function to get profit for himself out of that provision than it is a clergyman's function to get his stipend. This stipend is a due and necessary adjunct but not the object of his life if he be a true clergyman, any more than his fee (or honorarium) is the object of life to a true physician. Neither is his fee the object of life to a true merchant.[21]

The dignity of such work is clear and the humility of this relationship to remuneration offers a compelling antidote to the myopic pursuit of financial wealth and profit at the expense of, or with an indifference toward, cultural wealth and communal health.

What might we learn about bookselling from Ruskin's merchant? He tells us that "the merchant's first object in all his dealings must be (the public believe) to get as much for himself and leave as little to his neighbor or customer as possible . . . proclaiming vociferously, for law of the universe, that a buyer's function is to cheapen, and a seller's to cheat."[22] We have already discussed how Amazon, while it sells books—and sells more books than any other entity in the country, and more than all independent bookstores combined—is certainly not a bookseller; nor, as it turns out, is Amazon a merchant, as Ruskin defines the class. We have long known that Amazon sees books as its loss leader, a view that, in devaluing an entire industry devoted to creating cultural, not merely economic, value, reflects an unimaginably philistine way to turn a profit.

A loss leader is still a good deal for the consumer, if all one is measuring is a onetime consumer cost. Our merchant, as described by Ruskin, "has to apply all his sagacity and energy to the producing or obtaining it in the perfect state, and distributing it at the cheapest possible price where it is most needed."[23] Perhaps Amazon has it right then. After all, it is perceived to be distributing books at the cheapest possible price. But Ruskin's is not an argument for cheap prices as the primary goal of the merchant. He explicitly argues against one of Amazon's great competitive advantages (if you can call it that): the devaluing of the work that goes into the creation of the product to be provided. Acknowledging the vast networks required to produce any commodity, Ruskin writes that upon the merchant

> falls, in great part, the responsibility for the kind of life they lead; and it becomes his duty not only to be always considering how to produce what he sells, in the purest and cheapest forms, but how to make the various employments involved in the production . . . most beneficial to the men employed.[24]

Ruskin's low price isn't cheap—it's honest about the work required to create the product and the profits required to remunerate the full supply chain.

In addition, the service provided varies widely in certain professions, as well as under certain conditions in which price is not the primary consideration in the transaction. "We do not sell our prime-ministership by Dutch auction," Ruskin writes; when we are sick,

> we do not inquire for a physician who takes less than a guinea; litigious, we never think of reducing six-and-eightpence to four-and-sixpence; caught in a shower, we do not canvass the cabmen, to find

one who values his driving at less than a sixpence a mile.[25]

Amazon and others who sell books so cheaply as to render the profession of bookseller nearly extinct are not winning some sort of fair competition wherein the market dictates winners and losers. Certainly, the consumer should pay what they think a service or product is worth, and "the good workman employed, and the bad workmen unemployed." But systems like Amazon's are false, unnatural, and destructive, Ruskin tells us, when "the bad workman is allowed to offer his work at half-price, and either take the place of the good, or force him by his competition to work for an inadequate sum."[26]

Our merchants, especially our mass merchants, and especially our mass merchants who utilize one of the most essential tools for building humans and society, books (and the inquiry, discourse, arguments, beauty, and understanding contained therein), as loss leaders have fallen sway to "perhaps the most insolently futile [idea] that ever beguiled men through their vices": that wealth can be gained "irrespectively of the consideration of its moral sources."[27]

. . .

The booksellers' work is not exclusively, or, I would argue, primarily, retail work. In other words, their labor won't be duly compensated by the margins of book sales alone. The merchant's work, certainly as described by Ruskin, is noble and dignified, but it simply doesn't apply to booksellers. They are providing great cultural labor, these transcendental readers, these professors of books. They are providing what Hyde calls "gift labors." He asks how those who practice gift labors might nourish themselves "in an age whose values are market values and whose commerce consists almost exclusively in the purchase and sale of commodities."[28]

He knows the answer. He knows that there are models that can support such work. He says that, if we really valued gift labors, we could pay them well. "We could—we should—reward gift labors where we value them." His point here is "simply that where we do so we shall have to recognize that the pay [gift laborers] receive has not been 'made' the way fortunes are made in the market, that it is a gift bestowed by the group."[29] The market is well suited to cost-and-benefit analyses of easily quantifiable ends, especially when providers operate in an adversarial or competitive manner, but the costs and rewards of gift labor, Hyde explains, cannot be expressed through a market system.

The educator, the cleric, the artist, and the bookseller will never "make" money. Their larder, according to Hyde, will always be filled with gifts.

BODEGA AND BARROOM

Again, there is no good business model in the book industry, by which I mean there is no model to support books whose publication is driven by cultural and literary value rather than media attention and rapid sales. This is not new, of course, as de Bury's reflections show: "How shall the bargain be proved dear when the good that is purchased is infinite?"[30] The treasured wealth that good bookstores provide their community requires patience, a breadth of inventory, and a commitment to the readers idling in their literate confines, engaged in the loitering act of discovery known as browsing. And our booksellers—the good ones—are experts in the filtration, selection, assemblage, and enthusiasm required to stack the shelves with books whose value isn't measured by markets—and certainly not by short-term markets—alone. Our model should reward the work required of the bookseller that allows this sort of bookstore to flourish.

In the spring of 1980, the novelist E. L. Doctorow appeared before the U.S. Senate Committee on the Judiciary, making a similar case on behalf of books. The committee was conducting hearings on the book industry, specifically the consolidation of publishers and media companies. Doctorow, then vice president of the American Center of PEN International, voiced great concern for mixing the business of sitcoms, sporting events, celebrity biographies, and other ephemeral entertainments with the unformulaic, untameable, unmeasurable, and seemingly useless labor needed for the publishing of great books. He concluded his statement thus: "Traditionally all the other media have stood toward our books as extenders, popularizers, commentators—but the impulse from the book precedes all."[31]

The commerce of books is incommensurate with the commerce engaged in by the media conglomerates. "That core of free uneconomic expression," Doctorow explained,

> is the source of our cultural wealth. Because of its central, prior, primal place, it must be left as uncontrolled, inefficient, wasteful, diverse, unstructured as possible, so that our genius in the multiple witness and conscience we make as a people can rise to our national benefit without constriction or censorship.[32]

There is a certain sort of commerce—unfortunately, the prevailing one—that is incommensurate with the writing of a certain sort of book, with publishing it, and with selling it.

• • •

We'll recall Morley's description of our inventory conundrum: we need to combine the functions of the barroom and the bodega. What is true of these publicans of bookselling is true of publishers as well, for booksellers are merely the last stop between the author and their reader; if not for prescient and committed publishers whose work dignifies the shelves of bookstores and libraries, there would be no good bookstores.

Peter Mayer, the legendary publisher of authors as diverse as J. M. Coetzee, Stephen King, Iris Murdoch, Terry McMillan, and Salman Rushdie,* reflected on the state of publishing in 1978. He too delighted in the complexity of the business. He offered a characteristically thoughtful and unapologetic defense of the right balance of cultural and financial pursuits, making a stirring business case for expanding our temporal measures of success. "A caring for books preeminent to a purely business concern," he tells us with merciful patience,

> is anything but an anti-business point of view. Instead, it is good business and only establishes *that the time-table for book publishing success may often be different from the time table of other industries viewed statistically.* . . . If everything is current figures, it is a nasty industry that will burst out of the egg. . . . Without an eye to the future, regardless of current figures, the resultant enterprise will not only be shoddy but also economically unpromising. . . . It is not that some enduring books will not be published, that some enduring writers will not be encouraged. It is rather that *the emphasis of each firm will be increasingly on the ephemeral* . . . and that the fortunes and energies and spirit of the firms and the people in them will be organized and oriented

---

* Mayer would be heroic in his moral clarity and fortitude around the publication and defense of Rushdie's *The Satanic Verses*.

to a ramshackle machine driving forward at ever greater speeds.[33]

While we may or may not see the business concern as a primary driver of this work, we do want to practice it with fiscal responsibility and a commitment to meeting and creating demand. Books require patience at every level—creating them, producing them, marketing them, selling them, and reading them. If we measure them alongside more ephemeral products, we will necessarily elevate books of the moment over books of all time.

Morley tells of an amateur bookseller at Boston's Old Corner Bookstore doing his part to sell as much literature, or what he deemed literature, as possible during the holiday season. In 1913, having sold quite a bit of Conrad, he was reproached by his more seasoned colleagues. The bookseller's job, they told him, "during the Christmas Rush . . . is to satisfy customers promptly; not to encourage them to loiter and litigate the niceties of belles lettres." But he too exhibited a patience worthy of his trade.

His Old Corner eureka the next year was Emily Dickinson, whose *The Single Hound* was brought out in 1914 by Little, Brown. That book marked the beginning of the rediscovery of the divine Emily, but it took close to fifteen years for it to become general. In the book business you can usually reckon that it takes at least ten years for work of any really subtle quality to become widely known.

That is not as regrettable as you might imagine: ten years is a fair mellowing period, and strong work does not easily evaporate.[34]

So much of our work is litigating the niceties, encouraging readers to loiter and linger, that they might have their own eureka. Yamazaki explains what is at stake when we don't allow a fair mellowing period. Booksellers and publishers can't support the work of authors like Toni Morrison, "whose first few books had sales under five thousand copies," if we respond only to initial sales figures. "This kind of thinking," he says, "creates an industry where a young editor who discovers someone they think can be a future Toni Morrison has no chance of doing that author's third or fourth book unless they have significant sales."[35]

It is said that the shelf life of a book at the legendary Gotham Book Mart in New York appeared to be "however long it takes for the person who is next destined to read the book to arrive at the shop and discover that it's there." A fundamental principle of life at Gotham Book Mart, or City Lights, or Source Booksellers, or any good bookstore, is that "books have destinies as objects, and people appointments with them."[36]

SOCKS AND BOOKS

There is a scarcity of good bookstores. A survey of the media devoted to independent bookstores belies this fact. According to the press, bookstores are, against

95

all odds, thriving at this late date, providing an ana-
log antidote to our virtual digital worlds. They are
doing this by focusing on what the Harvard Business
School professor Ryan Raffaelli, calls the "3C's": community, curation, and convening.[37]

Raffaelli spent eight years embedding himself in
the independent book industry. During that stretch
in the 2010s, the Seminary Co-op's sales grew by
27 percent, but its bottom line remained steady: an
annual deficit of approximately $300,000. Perhaps
there is a model, Raffaelli argues, that acknowledges
the wisdom of retail and provides fair remuneration.
With increased efficiency in handling the books,
paying staff at rates commensurate with retail and
service work (that is, minimum wage), supplement-
ing book revenue with products that carry higher
profit margins (say, socks or coffee—or candles, wine,
greeting cards, toys, calendars, and so on), and com-
mitting to only carrying books that will sell quickly
at high margins, the savvy bookseller just might eke
out a living.

This is the perspective not only of a sympathetic
business school professor, alas, but of some of the
most passionate and committed experts in the industry. In 2018, I made my best attempt to convince
Oren Teicher, then CEO of the American Booksellers
Association (ABA), that a serious bookstore in the
twenty-first century needs a new model, and that it's
likely that all good bookstores will need one too. He
told me that there is no reason that a bookstore of
Seminary Co-op's size (or any bookstore whose an-

nual revenue exceeds $750,000) shouldn't be able to expect "a modest return," perhaps 1 or 2 percent of the store's revenue as bottom-line profit. Perhaps we have just been doing it wrong.

The ABA compiles an annual survey called Abacus that measures the financial statements and operational metrics of the nation's independent booksellers. Raffaelli relies on these numbers, as does Teicher, who is using the Abacus metrics to make his point. Perhaps there is something worth considering here if, in fact, a well-run bookstore can expect—presuming certain measures are met—a modest return on its sales.

Certainly, there is some public relations benefit in speaking to our strength and celebrating our success as an industry. It's more palatable to back an industry in ascent than to arrest its demise. But there is tremendous danger in overstating the trend. "Whenever anyone begins to think about arts advocacy," Morrison writes in *The Source of Self-Regard*, "a complex obstacle presents itself at once: artists have a very bad habit of being resilient, and it is that resilience that deceives us into believing that the best of it sort of gets done anyhow—and the 'great' of that 'best' sort of lasts anyhow."[38] Morrison, writing about artists and arts organizations, could have been writing about so many other treasured institutions, including bookstores.

As soon as Teicher made his point, something was clarified for me, and I quantified in response. The bookstore identified in Teicher's and Raffaelli's models of a bookstore must meet the following criteria in order to be profitable:

- Nearly 20 percent of a bookstore's inventory must consist of products that are not books.
- The books that are carried must be mostly purchased from major presses that offer higher gross margins than small, independent, and scholarly presses.
- Bookstores must leave books on their shelves no longer than four months.
- Bookstores must pay booksellers the wages of an entry-level retail clerk.

Books, Raffaelli notes, have "razor-thin profit margins," and a serious bookstore like the Seminary Co-op could never achieve even these modest margins.[39] Books make up over 99 percent of our inventory, compared to an industry average of 81.7 percent. Our overall margins, deflated by our large selection of academic books, which have an even lower margin than books by mainstream presses, are 37.7 percent, compared to an industry average of 45.3 percent. We are patient with our books and deliberately maintain a large inventory, acknowledging that we are providing a browsing experience as much as selling any particular book. Our books sit on the shelf for 280 days, compared to an industry average of 132 days. High-turning inventory is a foundational principle of successful retail. And while we pay booksellers well below what we believe they are worth, we currently pay 29 percent above the average bookseller's salary. Ours is a deliberate strategy; clearly the model isn't built for us.

Allow me to restate: 18.3 percent of what the average independent bookstore stocks are what is known as sidelines, not books. While some of us appreciate being able to pick up a greeting card or a nice pair of socks when we're at a bookstore, the bookstore's decision to stock those items is not an idiosyncratic curatorial decision, but an economic necessity. Raffaelli speaks to this as a strength and a challenge, noting that, "because the profit margins on books are extremely thin, sidelines serve as an effective way to bolster store profitability."[40] "Bolster" is the wrong word. There is no profitability without sidelines. To eke out our extremely thin profit margins, booksellers must sell nonbook merchandise—whether socks or coffee, they cannot stock only books. We'll recall that Amazon is using books as loss leaders to attract consumers into its "suite" of more profitable products and services.

But shouldn't the impulse from the book precede all, as Doctorow exhorted? If so, it is clear that we aren't doing it wrong. The business model has failed us, not we it. We need to build a model that supports a vast, slow-selling inventory of books—just books—deliberately assembled to provide even the most world-weary reader with a browse that surprises and delights. Our model must find ways to achieve the metrics that indicate a commitment to books—serious books—offered for sale with a patience worthy of cultural artifacts.

One year after my conversation with Teicher, recognizing that there was no place for us in the prevailing model of the financially sustainable bookstore, the Seminary Co-op established the model of the not-for-profit bookstore whose mission is bookselling. Rather than rely on the retail model—buying cheap and selling dear—our new model looks to financing from the gift economy to provide an articulation of the sort of work we are attempting. Our society struggling to be born might build good bookstores in its communities if it understood the great value of a bookstore's gifts.

VALUE AND WORTH

The most important things in the world seem impossible to measure. We have as yet, as Carlyle said, no scale to measure admiration by.[41] And we have as yet no scale for measuring meaning, knowledge, hope, pleasure, reverence, curiosity, beauty, kindness, awe, justice, wisdom, and love.

Not everything need be quantified. Sophisticated as social scientists' methods have become, and as valuable as their work is, we know how limiting metrics can be. Anyone who has dreamed of something like the Utilitarian Jeremy Bentham's felicific calculus, his scientific system for measuring happiness—in other words, for measuring the unmeasurable—understands how the precision of measure and the significance of the measured are in inverse proportion to each other. The fact that these qualities are unmeasurable and unquantifiable, that they respond to a personal, subjective scale, is, perhaps, integral to their meaning.

Measurement in and of itself isn't necessarily the problem. The problem is a reliance on measure over experience and on the quantifiable over the qualifiable. Again Musil helps us here. In his 1922 essay "Helpless Europe," he makes a distinction between morality and ethics. "In accord with its prescriptive nature, morality is tied to experiences that can be replicated, and these are precisely what characterize rationality as well, for a concept can only take hold in areas where explicitness and, figuratively speaking, replicability obtain." In matters of meaning, however, replicability is an absurd notion.

> Thus there exists a profound connection between the civilizing character of morality and of the scientific spirit, whereas the truly ethical experience, such as love, introspection, or humility, is, even where it is of a social nature, something difficult to transmit, something quite personal and almost antisocial.[42]

Perhaps we should implement alternative models for which we have fashioned more subtle scales that require developing our eloquence as qualifiers, not just our accuracy as quantifiers. These alternatives need not entirely replace the prevailing systems of economics and politics. If our societal goal is to make homo economicus a more rational actor and homo civicus a more enlightened citizen, then we must acknowledge that our systems have been indisputably ineffective.

EDUCATED AND LEARNED

"It is one thing to wish to utilize knowledge," Alexis de Tocqueville writes, "and another to wish for pure knowledge."[43] I'd like to consider two alternative models in two different types of academies, both of which aspire to provide the learned with a structure best suited to pure inquiry for its own sake: the kollel and the Institute for Advanced Study (IAS) in Princeton. While neither of these institutions would translate wholly into bookselling—and neither is without its issues—taken together they might offer instructive ways to challenge underlying assumptions about our current financial model for bookselling.

Beth Medrash Govoha, the largest kollel in the United States, is thirty miles southeast of Princeton in Lakewood, New Jersey. Its physical proximity to the Institute for Advanced Study is a coincidence, but the two institutions share certain values about learning for its own sake and supporting scholars who are pursuing unfettered scholarship.

Rabbi Judah bar Ilai, in the second century, lamented the state of the current generation:

The former generations made the study of Torah their regular concern and their daily work their occasional concern, and they succeeded in the one and in the other. The recent generations have made their daily work their regular concern and their study of Torah their occasional concern, and they have succeeded neither in the one nor in the other.[44]

The contemporary kollel, by acknowledging that the financial support of scholars studying Torah is a means by which those who are consumed by their daily work can help lift up the community, has found an elegant solution to the question of value and worth.

In the Orthodox Jewish community, the study of Torah (and, by extension, Talmud) is of the utmost importance. Shammai tells us to "make your study of Torah a regular practice."[45] Ben Bag Bag says, "Turn to it, and turn to it again, for everything is in it. Pore over it, grow old and gray over it. Do not budge from it. You can have no better guide for living than it."[46] And Rabbi Yochanan ben Zakkai was wont to say, "If you have studied much Torah, don't take credit for yourself, as that is what you were created to do."[47]

The descendants of Rabbi Judah bar Ilai understand that not everyone is created with the same appetite or facility for study. They see wisdom in a model whereby some community members make their daily work their regular concern so that other community members might make the study of Torah their regular work. In this way, the entire community is sanctified by Torah study. They call this arrangement the Yissachar-Zebulun partnership, after two of Jacob's thirteen children, whose eponymous tribes supposedly operated in this way: Zebulun committed to daily work and Yissachar committed to studying Torah.

The IAS, founded in 1930 by Abraham Flexner, was "intended to be a 'paradise for scholars' with no students or administrative duties,"[48] according to its current director, Robbert Dijkgraaf. The IAS attracted great scholars and thinkers and created an environment where they could "fully concentrate on deep thoughts, as far removed as possible from everyday matters and practical applications. It was the embodiment of Flexner's vision of the 'unobstructed pursuit of useless knowledge,' which would only show its use over many decades, *if at all*."[49]

The IAS's founding and continued existence (it has since served as a model for other such institutes throughout the world) is an argument on behalf of study for its own sake, regardless of utility. It is a shrine to human inquiry, reflecting "Flexner's lifelong conviction that human curiosity, with the help of serendipity, was the only force strong enough to break through the mental walls that block truly transformative ideas and technologies." According to Dijkgraaf, Flexner "believed that only with the benefit of hindsight could the long arcs of knowledge be discerned, often starting with unfettered inquiry and ending in practical applications."[50]

Even if "pure knowledge" were to prove utterly useless, Flexner, de Tocqueville, and Rabbi Judah bar

Ilai would commit to its pursuit all the same as an end in itself. That the pursuit of "useless knowledge," on occasion, has created some of our most world-changing insights, inventions, and scientific discoveries almost subverts the purity of the endeavor. Dijkgraaf tells us that

> Flexner himself admitted that basic research would inevitably waste some money but that the successes would far outweigh the failures. There is no direct or predictable link between the quality of basic research and its effect. The time scales can be long, much longer than the four-year periods in which governments and corporations nowadays tend to think, let alone the twenty-four-hour news cycle. It can easily take many years, even decades, or sometimes, as in the case of Einstein's theory of relativity, a century, for the full societal value of an idea to come to light.[51]

Flexner celebrates "curiosity, which may or may not eventuate in something useful," calling it the "outstanding characteristic of modern thinking."[52]

Michael Faraday, the nineteenth-century scientist whose perspective inspired Flexner, did not care to answer the question of utility. "Any suspicion of utility," Flexner writes, "would have restricted his restless curiosity. In the end, utility resulted, but it was never a criterion to which his ceaseless experimentation could be subjected."[53] Dante went so far as to say that these utilitarians "should not be considered as men of letters, since they do not acquire learning for its own sake but only to gain money or honors; just as we would not consider someone a lyre player if he kept a lyre in order to hire it out, instead of playing it."[54]

The great aphorist E. M. Cioran wrote a Socratic midrash that might serve as an extreme illustration of this point. "While they were preparing the hemlock, Socrates was learning how to play a new tune on the flute. 'What will be the use of that?' he was asked. 'To know this tune before dying.'" There needn't be any additional justification; to Cioran's mind, whether studying on the brink of death or in any other moment, there is no other justification of aspiration to knowledge; it is "the sole serious justification of any desire to know, whether exercised on the brink of death or at any other moment of existence."[55]

MORALITY AND ETHICS

Dare we imagine a secular counterpart to the Yissachar-Zebulun partnership—a model that would acknowledge the tremendous value of our cultural, literary, and intellectual heritage? Certainly, within a society that created museums, public universities, free libraries, and great concert halls exists a sensibility, an appetite for such imagination. Liesl Olson, writing of Chicago's second renaissance, for instance, speaks to the "Progressive era belief in high culture as a means of civic and moral uplift." She writes that "a sense of noblesse oblige underwrote the financial backing of many of Chicago's powerful cultural institutions," including institutions like the University of Chicago, the Newberry Library, and the Art Institute.[56]

The remarkable thing about the Yissachar-Zebulun partnership is the inversion of the nobility that is obligated in the noblesse oblige. Zebulun is not offering charity to Yissachar, whose study elevates the community, but providing financing for something that is considered both priceless and unworthy of credit, for it is what we are created to do. The nobility is Yissachar's—his obligation to study on behalf of poor Zebulun.

•   •   •

It behooves us to recall that we created these models, and we erred. We might yet rectify the error. With Ruskin, "I do not doubt the conclusions of the science if its terms are accepted." Like him,

> I am simply uninterested in them, as I should be in those of a science of gymnastics which assumed that men had no skeletons. It might be shown on that supposition that it would be advantageous to roll the students up into pellets, flatten them into cakes, or stretch them into cables; and that when these results were affected, the reinsertion of the skeleton would be attended with the conclusions true, and the science deficient only in applicability. Modern political economy stands on a precisely

similar basis. It imagines that man has a body but no soul to be taken into account and frames its laws accordingly. How can such laws possibly apply to man in whom the soul is the predominant element?[57]

Our political economy must make the distinction between worth and value, learned and educated, ethics and morality. We must embrace multiple measures, and the experiences and sensations for which we have no measure at all, giving each their proper due. In this way, we might build a model that returns the skeleton to the gymnast.

CHAPTER FOUR

Community

Books feed and cure and chortle and collide.
—GWENDOLYN BROOKS, *Very Young Poets*, 27

THE ACCESS OF PERFECTION TO THE PAGE

There is something solemn about mornings, when the world is quiet and the shop is calm. The books are illuminated by a dim natural light. When empty, the bookstore is filled with community, with our collective memory—with aspiration both communal and individual—and when full, the bookstore often maintains a quiet usually obtainable only in solitude. The arguments and enthusiasms contained in the volumes on the shelves create their own communion with the individual reader, while also providing a mechanism for discourse. It is a public square, no less articulate for most often being mute.

William James writes of "our mental life, like a bird's life . . . made of an alternation of flights and perchings."[1] There is also a flight-and-perching rhythm to our balance of solitude and community. Our reflections in solitude and our engagement with community energize each other and propel insight forward. In book-filled rooms, solitude and community are simultaneously present.

The poet Charles Simic, at daybreak, after a night of "struggling to grasp the always elusive," finds insight on the pages of Heidegger: "No thinker has ever entered into another thinker's solitude."[2] And yet it is from this solitude that books are created and books are read; the book created by the solitary thinker allows us to enter their thoughts, as our reading in solitude invites us to think in communion.

We find further insight in Stevens's poem where "the reader becomes the book":

The house was quiet because it had to be.

The quiet was part of the meaning, part of the mind:
The access of perfection to the page.[3]

And the world was calm.

• • •

We enter a bookstore for many reasons, in many moods. We enter a bookstore settled, but the ideas we encounter unsettle us. The company, however, is comforting and the connection provides a pleasant stirring.

We enter a bookstore unsettled, hoping to settle something within us. The arguments across the shelves further unsettle us, but it is not an unpleasant stirring. As reading became his passion as a young man, Richard Wright's books created moods in which he lived for days.[4] We understand what Wright meant.

In the privacy of our own minds, when the external din is quieted, when the prevailing opinions and judgments (which resemble conscience, but function mostly as pernicious censors) are silenced, we discover our own voices. We bring these voices back to the public square that we might, in the words of a Seminary Co-op bookseller describing the ethos of the store, "trouble easy consensus."

• • • •

"The Seminary Co-op Bookstore," writes the prolific author Cass Sunstein, "is not merely a bookstore. It is a community."[5] The sociologist Morris Janowitz, who helped finance the original Powell's bookstore, "believed in bookstores because he believed in community, and bookstores built community." Sunstein, on a similar tip, thought the Co-op "was analogous to a great city, as Jane Jacobs memorably described it: full of life-altering surprises and unknown treasures, and whenever you turned a corner, you never knew what you would see."[6] Sunstein and Janowitz both understood that a good bookstore reflects its community, but an exceptional bookstore both reflects and creates its community.

Jamie Kalven, the first-born son of the legal scholar Harry Kalven Jr., joined the Co-op in 1978. In the late 1980s, wanting to document the creation of his community, Kalven began work on a book that, in depicting a community "by way of the bookstore," would provide "a portrait of a village of readers." Kalven profiled a vast cross-section of the store's customers, including those he described as children just learning to read, exiled intellectuals, adult illiterates, great scholars at the frontier of their field,* celebrated writers, and passionate readers of all ages and backgrounds.[7] He was convinced that a key to understanding a community—in this case, his community on the South Side of Chicago—was understanding the citizens of the bookstore.

While this might seem like a disparate group, they are all a certain type of intellectual ambler: their thoughts roam while browsing; carried through the store by their shuffling feet, they scan the shelves in some sort of focused meditation. They recognize each other as they gather books they have never heard of and would have never imagined they wanted if they had heard of them. They surprise themselves in realizing this was just the sort of book they were hoping to find. "Something there is in the float of the sight of things," as Whitman says, "that provokes it out of the soul."[8] And these amblers trust the intuitions that arise while wandering the stacks.

---

* One of the great scholars Kalven interviewed was our friend Edward Shils, whose 1963 essay on the bookshop helped Kalven formulate some of his own ideas about the bookstore as community institution.

It is perhaps this class of reader that one of our longtime members, a professor of history at the University of Oklahoma, had in mind when he told me that the Co-op allows him to see and to keep a piece of the truly beautiful, offering thanks from "the quiet, bookish thousands." "It's a lonely world out here." He signed off, "On to haying."

CUSTOMER SERVICE FOR SOLITAIRES

Lest booksellers forget whom they serve, the prevailing model of exceptional customer service in American retail—knowledgeable, solicitous, effervescent, a bit breathless in a desire to serve, dignified and measured in expressing gratitude for the customers' decision to support this business over another—while often preferable to its smug, enervated, or dour alternatives, and more than occasionally a palpable good in itself, must be adapted for bookstores. To operate a good bookstore, the bookseller, as they establish an ethos of service, understands that the disposition of the solitaire must be considered.

We are aware that some of our customers might want help or a kindly greeting from a bookseller, but just as many will insist on a certain decorum whereby we disturb the bookstore code of silence only after an invite from the patron. While those who need help deserve the same swift, knowing, and affable engagement they might expect to receive across any other service counter—say, at a hardware store—the bookseller must recognize that it is the company of books, more than the company of book-sellers, that brings readers into the shop, at least at first.

"The Co-op staff understands what a serious activity browsing is," Kalven observes. "It seems to be an unspoken principle that customers carry into the store the privacy that encloses the act of reading. The staff stands ready to help, but they do not bear down on you." It is a space, he continues, "at once utterly private and convivial."[9] Even dear friends spying each other across the store feel that a greeting would be an intrusion—it can wait, they tell themselves, for a less private setting.

This is how the browser recognizes their book: privately, usually in silence, "for often the most important books are shy, and do not press forward to the front counters," as Morley observes.[10] We must maintain quiet and allow for concentrated browsing, understanding that our role is drawing readers across the threshold, that they might confront these volumes. If, after all, shades are to be dislodged, the tactics used to sell everything from mattresses to vitamins to pickaxes might not be the tactic best deployed in the stacks.

• • •

Kalven must have read his Mauss, his Sahlins, his Hyde. "Booksellers necessarily operate in two economies," he writes: "the gift economy of passions and soul hunger and the market economy in which books are commodities."[11]

Books *and* bookstores are often gifts, not commodities, as Hyde differentiates. "It is the cardinal difference between gift and commodity exchange that a gift establishes a feeling-bond between two people, while the sale of a commodity leaves no necessary connection." Just about any bookseller, and most bookstore patrons, will tell you tales of the human connections solidified over the sale of books. In retail, it needn't be this way. Besides, it's not even possible in most exchanges. In further explaining the distinction, Hyde takes us into the hardware store to buy a hacksaw blade; we promptly leave. He feels no connection with the clerk and is indifferent to whether or not he will see the clerk again. "The disconnectedness," he reminds us, "is, in fact, a virtue of the commodity mode. We don't want to be bothered. If the clerk always wants to chat about the family, I'll shop elsewhere. I just want a hacksaw blade. But a gift makes a connection."[12]

One Co-op customer sent me a laudatory email, praising the service he received, including great conversation with the booksellers. He went on to recommend that we institutionalize the bookseller as a conversationalist, not recognizing how common the spontaneous book discussion is in these parts. He thought that the occasional appearance of a wandering troubadour "who liked to talk about books and a wide range of topics would enliven the experience of being in the bookstore and might

stimulate book sales." He didn't realize just how fre-
quently such conversation arises. In fact, it is not
only booksellers who hold forth on books and ideas
in our store but customers too, expressing their enthusiasms and aversions, airing their responses to
the books of the moment and the books of all times,
and sharing their attempts at answering unanswer-
able questions. There is something about the depths
of the connection through books, be they bonds of
curiosity, literature, or ideas, that elicits uncommon
and edifying intimacies.

· · ·

The book and bookstores are both gifts that can operate in commodity mode for those who prefer it. After
all, sometimes we just need a book. While I happen
to enjoy chatting with clerks, even while purchasing
a hacksaw, and find pleasure in establishing connections with casual acquaintances, Hyde's point holds:
there is no *necessary* connection in the commodity
exchange. In these cases, the exercise of knowledge,
efficiency, affability, and a degree of anonymity are
all demanded of the bookseller.

How to balance privacy and conviviality, solitude
and engagement, within a bookstore? How might we
activate that alternating current so as to generate the
energy required to take that long journey inward?
The good bookseller perpetually considers this question, and the good bookstore gets the balance right
most of the time.

THE COMPANY OF THE SOLITARY READER

"The pleasantest of all diversions," according to Kenkō, a fourteenth-century Buddhist priest, "is to sit alone under the lamp, a book spread out before you, and to make friends with people of a distant past you have never known."[13] We have felt the companionship of books, and we find in their pages a companionship that our authors felt in the presence of their books. "Laurence Sterne's neighbors think him 'often alone' when he is in fact 'in company with more than five hundred mutes' who, when summoned, will communicate their ideas to him by dumb signs."[14]

Books offer consolation, nourishment, and care. Machiavelli, upon entering his study, was "welcomed lovingly by them." He fed upon the food which was his own, he tells us, and "for which [he] was born," sounding like a *talmid chacham*.[15] William Hazlitt, "with a few old authors," somehow managed "to get through the summer or winter months, without ever knowing what it is to feel *ennui*."[16] They sat with him at breakfast and walked with him before dinner.

Sterne derived "a peculiar satisfaction in conversing with the ancient and modern dead,—who yet live and speak excellently in their works."[17] In our time, the poet and critic Mary Ruefle tells us that she "began writing because [she] had made friends with the dead": "they had written to me, in their books, about life on earth and I wanted to write back and say *yes, house, bridge, river, hair, no, maybe, never, forever*."[18]

We readers have felt the companionship of books, and many of us have found ourselves at a loss to explain to the underliterate among us the power and nourishment we receive from our books. "These friends of mine," Petrarch says of the uninitiated, "regard the pleasures of the world as the supreme good; they do not comprehend that it is possible to renounce these pleasures." Moreover,

they are ignorant of my resources. I have friends whose society is delightful to me; they are persons of all countries and of all ages; distinguished in war, in council, and in letters; easy to live with, always at my command. They come at my call, and return when I desire them: they are never out of humor, and they answer all my questions with readiness. Some present in review before me the events of past ages; others reveal to me the secrets of Nature: these teach me how to live, and those how to die: these dispel my melancholy by their mirth, and amuse me by their sallies of wit: and some there are who prepare my soul to suffer everything, to desire nothing, and to become thoroughly acquainted with itself. In a word, they open a door to all the arts and sciences.[19]

And what do they ask in return? What sort of care do they need? "As a reward for such great services, they require only a corner of my little house, where they may be safely sheltered from the depredations of their enemies.* In fine, I carry them with me into the fields, the silence of which suits them better than the business and tumults of cities."[20] It is imperative that we booksellers be capable of maintaining the silence that will suit, it seems, both the volumes and their conscientious readers, once they have been properly introduced.

• • •

Given the gifts we receive from these wise and humble companions, is it any wonder that we feel such affection for them? Leigh Hunt, who liked to lean his head against a book, making physical contact, was a friend to our friend Charles Lamb. He reflected thus:

I looked sideways at my Spenser, my Theocritus, and my Arabian Nights; then above them at my Italian poets; then behind me at my Dryden and Pope, my romances, and my Boccaccio; then on my left side at my Chaucer, who lay on a writing-desk; and thought how natural it was in C. L. to give a kiss to an old folio, as I once saw him do to Chapman's Homer.[21]

You might recall that, for my ancestors and their descendants, with their ornate volumes, this is daily ritual. The Jewish custom upon closing a sacred

* "Books have the same enemies as man: fire, moisture, animals, the weather—and what's inside them" (Valéry, *Analects*, 95).

book is to kiss the cover with *kavana* (intention), as a gesture of respect and affection.

EVERY READER THEIR OWN REBBE

Just as my grandfather and his community went to the basement of his shul, Bnei Yehuda, on the corner of Sixteenth Avenue and Fifty-Third Street to learn with their *chevrusa*, so I and mine, for generations, reported to the basement of the Chicago Theological Seminary on the corner of Fifty-Eighth Street and University Avenue, to learn with our friends, living and dead. Like my grandfather, we then repaired to our personal libraries to find our own perspective, buttressed by and in relation to the conversations we held. We were galvanized by the alternating current of solitude and community.

I was raised in a tradition in which all readers not only engaged the same texts, but engaged the same texts at the same time. Every week of the year had its prescribed Torah portion, and every day of the year had its page of Talmud, the *daf yomi.** Every observant Jew the world over could read that same portion and study that same page. The binding element of such unified study cannot be overstated. In every community, in every shul, heads swayed over

* The literal translation is "page of the day." The *Daf Yomi* program was instituted in the early twentieth century by the Lubliner Rav, Yehuda Meir Shapiro.

the same page of the same book. Every seven and a half years, a global celebration was held over the completion of 63 books in 2,711 days.

But such orthodoxy is for the faithful, and I am seduced by the heresy of intellectual heterodoxy. Besides, there is so much to read, and I only have 750 books left, if I'm lucky.

• • •

The Hebrew word for heretic, *apikores*, is derived from the Aramaic transliteration of the name Epicurus. Its meaning might be in response to the philosopher's teachings, including the teaching that the gods exist but are unknowable by us and indifferent to us, a supposition that liberates us from trying to understand them. Epicurus would have us turn to that which can be discerned: the mortal natural world, our own minds, how we spend our time, and how we treat each other.

Or, perhaps, the word *apikores* is derived from the word *hefker*, meaning freedom. Either way, for someone who grew up in the Talmudic tradition, who understood the beauty of this particular instantiation of the Jewish way of life, my heresy is liberating and branded with an Epicurean epithet.

And what does that freedom afford the *apikores*? How can the *apikores*, following Epicurus's teachings, find friendship and the pleasure derived from prudence—from seeing things as they are? The *apikores* can discover such community in book-lined rooms where everyone is their own rebbe, creating their own plans for a *daf yomi*, perhaps in small *chevrusas*, perhaps in solitude, but always in dialogue with scores of authors living or dead who might have something to say about the topic at hand.

And so I, along with the legion secular *talmidim*, build my own private Talmud—commentaries on how to be a human—from the shelves of good bookstores. "*Your* classic author," Calvino tells us, "is the one you cannot feel indifferent to, who helps you to define yourself in relation to him, even in dispute with him."[22] What is our personal canon but the building of community—our elective affinities?

The varieties of assemblages reflect a great democratic principle: in this way, and perhaps only in this way, do we fully choose what the literary critic and Co-op enthusiast Wayne Booth called "the company we keep." Gatekeepers are relieved of their duty as we consider the works of thinkers, poets, and novelists in the privacy of our own thoughts. We program our own symposia, and we call on only the best minds.

"We may hear," as does Tennyson, "the voice of Demosthenes, Homer, or *Roman Virgil*," or, with Milton, "sweetest Shakespeare, Fancy's child, Warble his native wood-notes wild."[23] We are like Petrarch, for whom, according to Tatham, "Cicero, Seneca and Augustine were individuals in whom he discerned the reflection of his own personality, and, as he read their works, he held long and animated dialogues with them."[24]

We may hear, beside Holbrook Jackson, "Burke perorate at Westminster, Johnson dogmatize in Fleet Street, Socrates argue, Rabelais laugh, Augustine confess, Swift scoff, Pepys gossip, Donne preach, Carlyle scold, Ruskin lecture, Taylor pray, Scott yarn, Herrick sing, Whitman sound his barbaric yawp, Shelley beat in the void his luminous wings in vain."[25]

Kenkō would choose "the moving volumes of *Wen Hsüan*, the collected works of Po Chü-i, the sayings of Lao Tzu, and the chapters of Chuang Tzu."[26]

Hazlitt thought of it a bit more literally: "I can 'take mine ease at mine inn,' beside the blazing hearth, and shake hands with Signor Orlando Friscobaldo, as the oldest acquaintance I have. Ben Jonson, learned Chapman, Master Webster, and Master Heywood are there; and seated round, discourse the silent hours away."[27]

For my part, I might hope to hear Lao Tzu clarify, Heraclitus mystify, Shankara discriminate, or Kenkō share whatever nonsensical thoughts have entered his head. On another evening, I might invite Epictetus and James Baldwin to cudgel, Susan Sontag and Johann Wolfgang von Goethe to speak from on high, Michel de Montaigne and Annie Dillard to wander, Ghalib and Lucille Clifton to tune their instruments, Martin Buber and Simone Weil to confront the divine, or Elisha ben Abuya and Friedrich Nietzsche to defeat it.

Perhaps I might "take mine ease at mine inn," where conversations abound. Langston Hughes and Richard Wright inspire Gwendolyn Brooks, and

123

she in turn influences Haki Madhubuti and Angela Jackson, who in turn teach Nate Marshall and Eve Ewing; the students lift up their mentors. Velimir Khlebnikov, Anna Akhmatova, Osip Mandelstam, and Marina Tsvetaeva, at the height of their talent, write their way through hopelessness; the hopelessness is justified by history, but I meet them when they are still young enough to believe that poetry can save them. Confucius challenges Lao Tzu, and Lao Tzu replies with the tongue of an immortal. Diogenes jeers at Alexander and Plato, trampling their pride. Robert Musil, Thomas Mann, Martin Buber, and Rainer Maria Rilke echo each other as they all try to balance precision and soul. Gertrude Stein confounds William James with her brilliance in the classroom and then goes on to lead one of the most exacting and least legible writing workshops; the students can't keep pace with their mentor.

Bookstores have long served as a great succor for those contending with loneliness. The great underappreciated poet Edwin Thomason's wry, half-serious challenge of a proclamation—that loneliness is immoral—resonates.

• • •

Emerson read the verses "of the great English poets, of Chaucer, of Marvell, of Dryden, with the most modern joy,—with a pleasure . . . which is in great part caused by the abstraction of all *time* from their verses." When we consider the fundamental concerns of humanity—love, suffering, meaning, wonder, a desire to understand, to connect, to make it all worthwhile—we realize that we are coeval with all writers whose books met these profound concerns with an answering profundity. "There is some awe mixed with the joy of our surprise," Emerson continues, "when this poet, who lived in some past world, two or three hundred years ago, says that which lies close to my own soul, that which I also had wellnigh thought and said." Which leads Emerson to the conviction "that one nature wrote and the same reads."[28]

How many inchoate books, in-progress books, tumescent books, unfinished books are carried by the browsers through our bookstores? We are all wandering the shelves with books, written and unwritten, in our heads. Unlike Emerson's "meek young men," who "grow up in libraries, believing it their duty to accept the views which Cicero, which Locke, which Bacon, have given; forgetful that Cicero, Locke, and Bacon were only young men in libraries when they wrote these books," we have heard what "the Arabian proverb says, 'A fig-tree, looking on a fig-tree, becometh fruitful.'"[29]

To make books, one must read books. Flaubert, in an extreme example, claims to have "absorbed" 1,500 books in order to write *Bouvard and Pécuchet*, a novel that speaks directly to the folly of completism and our vain search for encyclopedic knowledge.[30]

The writer wanders the stacks with books in their head and hands, finding community within the pages of the books on the shelf. Whether living or dead—a matter of indifference—the authors are immortalized. Hunt tells us "how pleasant it is to reflect, that all these lovers of books have themselves become books! What better metamorphosis could Pythagoras have desired! How Ovid and Horace exulted in anticipating theirs!"[31]

The writer, upon completing their book, transcends their corporeal form. The reader has the sole power of revivifying the writer, who is a shade at rest, capable of being dislodged, even if, still living, they dislodge shades of their own.

• • •

Whitman asks much of us, his readers. He exhorts us in his poem "Poets to Come": "Arouse! for you must justify me." He continues:

I myself but write one or two indicative words for
    the future,
I but advance a moment only to wheel and hurry
    back in the
darkness.[32]

He goes further in his essay "Democratic Vistas," where he calls for a different sort of literature, not this "perpetual, pistareen, paste-pot work" we've inherited, but something more demanding of its readers, a more *active* approach to reading. "Books are to be call'd for, and supplied," he writes, on the assumption that the process of reading is not a half-sleep, but, in highest sense, an exercise, a gymnast's struggle; that the reader is to do something for himself, must be on the alert, must himself or herself construct indeed the poem, argument, history, metaphysical essay—the text furnishing the hints, the clue, the start or framework. Not the book needs so much to be the complete thing, but the reader of the book does.[33]

What does Whitman mean by the construction of the "poem, argument, history, metaphysical essay," if not the construction of the poetic and principled narrative one tells about oneself to oneself, the narrative one tells about the world to oneself and one's community, in an attempt to live a meaningful life? Emerson and Simic have told us how we read ourselves when we read others, how we find ourselves in dialogue with our own lives when we are in dialogue with others. "I require a You to become; becoming I, I say You," asserts Buber, adding, "All actual life is encounter."[34]

The Front Table, Lear told us, is "about confrontation."[35] Hovering over the Front Table, we say "you," we say "I."

AN ISLAND OF EQUALITY

Compared to the university and its library, the bookstore, with its open doors, is distinctly democratic. All readers have the same access, and the bookstore is a great leveler. The authors and professors, the autodidacts and the curious, those seeking entertainment, edification, information, and the subversive are all treated equally. They are scanning the shelves, burrowing in their books, and finding insight in the aisles. All are invited to join the honorable company of scholars, artists, and thinkers and are given permission to engage and argue with the works, regardless of their pedigree or specialty. All ideas are presented without filters, demanding only that the reader clarify the books through the alembic of their own sensibility.

The bookstore, like the public library, is an open institution. While there is a cost to taking volumes home, there is no cost for entry. Browsing and loitering are encouraged. I am one of the many bookstore browsers who spent uncounted hours wandering bookstores before I had the money to purchase the books I coveted.* I have measured my financial success by the sort of book I could afford. Used books and remainders marked my early career, new paperbacks once I established a regular paycheck, the occasional hardcover as my salary increased, and finally, and not without sacrificing other material goods, buying books as they strike me, new or used, hardcover or soft, doing what I can to maintain the

---

* "It is the enjoying, not the possessing, that makes us happy" (Montaigne, "Of the Inequality That Is Between Us," in *The Complete Essays of Montaigne*, 192).

right balance of what Calvino demands in our personal library of classics.

• • •

Who are we, these quiet, bookish thousands? We are Protestant, not Catholic. We know that our relationship to books and their authors needn't be mediated; ours is a doctrine of universal priesthood. We take the poet and essayist Hanif Abdurraqib's reflection on houses of worship seriously: "The gospel is, in many ways, whatever gets people in the door to receive whatever blessings you have to offer."[36]

We wander the stacks without priests. We find our own way. But we are in good company. The "children just learning to read" browse the same shelves Patti Smith and Barack Obama browsed. "Exiled intellectuals" navigate a flight path that intersects with the paths taken by Ocean Vuong, Hanif Abdurraqib, and Sandra Cisneros, while "passionate readers of all ages and backgrounds" engage the bookstore that entranced Susan Sontag, Fred Moten, Wendy Doniger, Martha Nussbaum, Slavoj Žižek, Zadie Smith, and Susan Howe.

In his book *Conversation*, Stephen Miller, who has written extensively on literary culture, writes of eighteenth-century British coffeehouses what could well be said of bookstores:

The mingling of different classes in coffeehouses also impressed many visitors. "What a lesson," the

Abbé Prévost said, "to see a lord, or two, a baronet, a shoemaker, a tailor, a wine-merchant, and a few others of the same stamp poring over the same newspapers. Truly coffee houses . . . are the seats of English liberty." . . . Londoners praised the coffee-house for being an island of equality in a sea of class.[37]

Kalven was wise to think that a portrait of his community would best be drawn from the denizens commingling in the bookstore. The space is democratizing, but there can also be something gentle about its environs that helps bind us to each other, despite our profound differences.

A local librarian whose devotion to the Seminary Co-op has led her to attempt to articulate the function of the bookstore, thought that the psychoanalyst Adam Phillips might be of help. Phillips writes that kindness "joins us to various and diverse other people. Kindness is extravagant."[38] Our librarian looked up the etymology of "extravagant" and saw that it came to us from the Latin, by way of Middle French. The word is composed of *extra*, "outside of," and *vagary*, "to wander or roam." She wrote to me of her findings:

I realized that books help you wander outside of yourself, which can help you to be kind, because it can help you see issues from another person's perspective. Wandering sounds like browsing. So, it makes me happy to think of wandering through the aisles as a journey of kindness, one that takes us beyond the narrow limits of the self.

Shils, who earlier helped us define the good bookshop—explaining that it is "a place for intellectual conviviality, and it has the same value as conversation . . . as a necessary part of the habitat of a lively intelligence in touch with the world"—has helped us identify the bookstore as binding agent and community builder.[39] But it is not only a meek kindness that we find in the public square. Kalven, writing of the Co-op, noted that while they might be ideological adversaries, antagonists "are at home in the bookstore—members (literally and figuratively) of something they both hold dear."

Epicurus values wisdom *and* friendship. The *chevrusa* I spoke of earlier is predicated on friendship, but the debates are fierce. They remain respectful—usually—and are conducted in the spirit of camaraderie in a common pursuit of truth. A dispute, a *machlokes*, is the currency of the Talmud, as the classic symposium is itself an argument of sorts.

RHYTHMS OF RESPECT

Our public discourse is not functional, where it exists at all. There are so few spaces for conversation and meaningful encounter. Sherry Turkle, the founder of the MIT Initiative on Technology and Self, writes of the "rhythms of respect" that true conversation yields:

> Public conversations give us a way to reclaim private conversations by modeling them, including how to show tolerance and genuine interest in what other people are saying. . . . People have long sensed that this kind of public conversation is crucial to our democracy.[40]

The good bookstore serves as one such place to hold explicit and tacit public conversation, whether a reader engages in a dialogue with a bookseller or another patron over a book or a selection of books in which they share an interest or through which they sort through different perspectives; gathers with others to listen to an author speak of their work; or, as is commonly experienced, finds that the engagement with the books alone provokes an internal dialogue, a shuffling of hunches, assumptions, and prejudices, bringing texture and insight to the far reaches of our ignorance.

The ability to question our own beliefs, to dwell in uncertainty, empathy, or curiosity, to pursue knowledge, beauty, and meaning unstintingly, so that we might make our best attempt at understanding, and to continually put ourselves in spaces that will challenge, not just echo, our assumptions, is an act of citizenship as much as its own individual reward.

In the bookstore, one had "an impression of the wholeness of intellectual discourse," Kalven writes, "a healing of the splintering of discourse that has taken place within universities." Acknowledging that the books themselves are often at war with one another, arguing stridently, in the strongest of language and with the highest of stakes about truth and consequences, there remains something restorative about the bookstore itself. As Kalven writes, "The place that houses all these contending visions and impassioned quarrels stands—in its quiet, cheerful, serious way—for the possibilities of understanding and conciliation." There is something to glean of the totality of human experience in a space comprising its varieties. The constellation composed by the good bookseller serves as a harmonizing force.

●　●　●

In 1967, a faculty committee at the University of Chicago issued "The Kalven Report on the University's Role in Political and Social Action"; its chair was Jamie Kalven's father, Harry. The committee conceived "its function as principally that of providing a point of departure for discussion" and utilized most of the report to declare, with certainty, the "great and unique role" the university plays in fostering the values of a society.

The university is not quite unique in this role, and it may be falling short of its ideals, as the younger Kalven argued, but the values outlined in the Kalven Report are excellent guiding principles for bookstores, public libraries, and other intellectual institutions committed to a common pursuit of the intellectual life. Replacing "the university" with "the bookstore," and "the faculty member or the individual student" with "the reader," we could proudly adopt the following principles:

> The mission of the [bookstore] is the discovery, improvement, and dissemination of knowledge. Its domain of inquiry and scrutiny includes all aspects and all values of society. A [bookstore] faithful to its mission will provide enduring challenges to social values, policies, practices, and institutions. By design and by effect, it is the institution which creates discontent with the existing social arrangements and proposes new ones.
>
> In brief, a good [bookstore], like Socrates, will be upsetting. The instrument of dissent and criticism is the individual [reader]. The [bookstore] is the home and sponsor of critics; it is not itself the critic. It is, to go back once again to the classic phrase, a community of scholars. To perform its mission in the society, a [bookstore] must sustain an extraordinary environment of freedom of inquiry and maintain an independence from political fashions, passions, and pressures. A [bookstore], if it is to be true to its faith in intellectual inquiry, must embrace, be hospitable to, and encourage the widest diversity of views within its own community.[41]

This diversity of viewpoints needn't separate and splinter us; if done right, this sort of public discourse in the public square of the bookstore can bind us together, creating a more civic-minded populace.

To be clear, the bookstore is not a place for everything. It is not the internet, wherein every idea or thought is given its space, regardless of quality, hatefulness, or mendacity. The selections of the bookseller must filter for quality and a certain set of standards—of course, what we exclude is as meaningful as what we include—that help create a discourse that is inclusive, intellectually honest, and cognizant of the multiple ways in which materials are used in the wide-ranging intellectual life—an impression of which, Kalven thought, the bookstore restores.

WE'RE ALL BOOKSELLERS NOW

If we are to build community, support the public square, and, perhaps for some, provide certain blessings in a book-lined house of worship, the responsibility for supporting a thriving serious bookstore must fall to all of us. We're all, we readers, booksellers now.

Mark Hansen, a professor of political science, former Seminary Co-op board member, and erstwhile farmer, speaks of the booksellers' "urgent need to cultivate readership"—to preach the gospel, so to speak. He writes:

The bookseller's passion—for books, for the experience of reading, for the culture of the written word—is a source of inspiration for readers. Even more important, it is a crucial support for readers as they convey their enthusiasm to their children, their students, their friends, and their associates. For we, the habitués of bookstores, the readers of books, the patrons of the book culture, must also be booksellers. We too must model our belief that books, among all the world's commodities, have special properties: the arguments, the narratives, the stories, and the poetry within. We must cultivate readers as farmers tend their fields.[42]

On to haying.

CHAPTER FIVE

Time

The hours of folly are measur'd by the clock,
but of wisdom: no clock can measure.

—WILLIAM BLAKE, "The Marriage of Heaven and Hell,"
in *The Complete Poetry and Prose of William Blake*, 36

A DUBIOUS STATE OF INNER HYGIENE

Seneca, in his first letter to Lucilius, explains how precious time is, imploring Lucilius to hold it in his grasp and make the most use of it. You will not die at once, he says, you are dying every day. Use your time wisely, for "nothing, Lucilius, is ours, except time." Continuing, he exclaims:

> What fools these mortals be! They allow the cheapest and most useless things, which can be easily replaced, to be charged in the reckoning, after they have acquired them; but they never regard themselves in debt when they have received some of that precious commodity,—time! And yet time is the one loan which even a grateful recipient cannot repay.[1]

Everyone is in such a hurry. We have more time than most of our ancestors, but we shouldn't confuse our commitment to efficiency with an appreciation of that "precious commodity,—time." We might find an analogue for our mania in Musil's reflection: "The thesis that the huge quantities of soap sold testify to our great cleanliness need not apply to the moral life, where the more recent principle seems more accurate, that a strong compulsion to wash suggests a dubious state of inner hygiene."[2] Elizabeth Hardwick writes of her age and ours that "time is just what our contemporary existence is determined to shorten." With her characteristic perspicacity, she observes that time is "that curious loss in a world of time-saving."[3] Our manic obsession with efficiency yields time that we immediately and frivolously consume, cheapening it rather than appreciating it.

While time is something we obsessively save, we don't seem to value immersive time. Hardwick, one of our best readers, laments that, by losing time, we lose "time-consuming reading."[4] We aren't hurrying in order to make time for more meaningful endeavors, it seems. With all the time we create, so to speak, how might we hope to expend it? One would think that the extra time our efficiency affords us could be a collective gift that helps us slow down, ruminate, and attempt to understand the world around us, each other, and ourselves.

Hardwick laments, not the loss of reading proper, but the way we have focused our reading efforts on "memo and summary," thus losing the value provided by what Mary Cappello calls "slow time." If I may take the liberty of replacing "lecture" with "browse" and "essay" with "bookstore," in Cappello's formulation, we can understand how the good bookstore serves as a reliable decelerant:

> The time of the [browse]—like all that is beautiful about [a bookstore's] ruminative spell—is slow time. We could call it the time *of* understanding, over and against the time it takes *to* understand. Barthes calls it "a kind of divine time," a time that is "just" (as in fair, and laced with freedom), or, as he defines it—a "(delicate, slow, benevolent) passage from one logic to another, from one body to another."[5]

The good bookstore fosters the expenditure of a certain kind of time: the slow time of the browse. It is the time we take, for instance, to single out which Clarice Lispector novel we would like to read next. Or the time we take, when our eye is first caught by the curious cover of Saint Augustine's *Confessions* on the Front Table, to read the jacket copy of the book and the first few pages. "Who will grant me repose?" he asks.[6]

It is the time in which we notice that there are not one but two new translations of *Confessions* alongside two new translations of Homer's *Odyssey*, two new collections of Albert Murray's writings, and a reissued volume of Pauli Murray's *Song in a Weary Throat* (which recalls the Pauli Murray biography we spotted on our last bookstore visit), all assembled on the Front Table in an effort to create, for the unhurried, serendipitous literary discoveries.

It is the time we take to speak with the bookseller behind the desk about the long-awaited translation of Fernando Pessoa's *Book of Disquiet* or about the helpful new Stuart Hall collections, a time when we learn that the bookseller is also excited about Weil's *Gravity and Grace*, the ambitious Murty Classical Library of India, and the University of Chicago Press's completion of its exceptional edition of Seneca's works. (It might be time to reread those letters to Lucilius.*)

Such discoveries take time. They happen by being in that space where we let ourselves submit to aimlessness. Sometimes the spine of a book will catch our eye as we are making our way to the register and we'll grab it on impulse, then buy it on the good authority of the bookseller. How miraculous it will seem, in retrospect, that we had never heard of Kate Zambreno and were fortunate enough to notice that gray spine as we were passing by! We relish these discoveries, as we relish the time in which we make them.

• • •

The novel, Hardwick tells us, depends on a more subtle time, a "spiritual and intellectual lengthen-

---

* Remember what Canetti tells us: true spiritual life consists in rereading.

ing, extending like a dream in which much is surrendered and slowly transformed." This is true of all great works of inquiry, as are the additional conditions that Hardwick ascribes to the reading of fiction: "tranquility, slow hours and days, the need to discover, through the imagination, what the world about us contained . . . curiosity about the most knotted as well as the simplest of human activities."[7]

Slow, or immersive, time—like the hour of the browse—makes us receptive to the memory of humanity; we are uninterested in the ephemera created by speed and efficiency. In the novel *Slowness*, Milan Kundera explores what he refers to as the "secret bond" between "the demon of speed" and forgetting, and between slowness and memory.

"In existential mathematics," Kundera writes, "experience takes the form of two basic equations: the degree of slowness is directly proportional to the intensity of memory; the degree of speed is directly proportional to the intensity of forgetting." First an illustration of the equations:

Consider this utterly commonplace situation: a man is walking down the street. At a certain moment, he tries to recall something, but the recollection escapes him. Automatically, he slows down. Meanwhile, a person who wants to forget a disagreeable incident he has just lived through starts unconsciously to speed up his pace, as if he were trying to distance himself from a thing still too close to him in time.[8]

Then a lament:

> Why has the pleasure of slowness disappeared?
> Ah, where have they gone, the amblers of yester-
> year? Where have they gone, those loafing heroes of
> folk song, those vagabonds who roam from one mill
> to another and bed down under the stars? Have
> they vanished along with footpaths, with grass-
> lands and clearings, with nature?[9]

We know where they are. We see them as they amble,
we booksellers. They behold the stars and the fruit
tree blossoms.

• • •

We might approach the browse as Emerson approached education. "Leave this military hurry," he
exhorted, "and adopt the pace of Nature. Her secret
is patience."[10] The good bookseller trusts that the
browser has patience enough to allow for the mellowing period that some books require to attain their full
vibrancy. After all, as Hyde writes in distinguishing
labor from work, the labor of bookselling also "sets
its own pace." Bookselling is an art, and art, Zadie
Smith notes, "takes time and divides it up as art sees
fit."[11] The bookseller then must also adopt the pace of
nature. After all, how but by deliberate patience might
the mellowing period be achieved? Again, the average
bookstore leaves books on its shelves for 132 days. At
the Seminary Co-op, we leave books on our shelves for

280 days, lest we remove them prematurely. They need the time to settle, the time to rise, the time to flourish.

The *chef*'s wisdom: time itself is an ingredient. Remember what we learned from the Gotham Book Mart: "Books have destinies as objects, and people appointments with them."[12]

We see the *chef* roaming through the store, palpating the books, removing the dust jackets to have a look at the cloth, smelling the glue, testing for ripeness ("ripeness is all!"[13]), knowing that certain works might take years to ripen for certain readers, and that books of all time have no expiration dates and are not given to rot.

Walter Benjamin, unpacking his library, remembered his Terentianus Maurus: "*Pro captu lectoris libelli habent sua fata.* Books have their fates according to the reader's capacity."[14] And they are worth the wait. Recall Solomon's proverb: "How good is a word rightly timed?"[15]

Just as each of the nearly 100 trillion cells in the human body has its own chronometer, the bookstore comprises books that also have chronometers.[16] As they come and go, these books compose the bookstore. Too often our impatience as retailers relegates books to the dustbin before the upper chamber of their hourglass has emptied.

• • •

The bookstore's appeal resembles what Conrad describes as the artist's appeal, which "is made to our less obvious capacities: to that part of our nature which, because of the warlike conditions of existence, is necessarily kept out of sight within the more resisting and hard qualities—like the vulnerable body within a steel armor." When we enter the bookstore, we remove that armor. We relinquish to-do lists and news cycles so that we might dwell in our curiosity and the profundity of the literary and intellectual sensibility. The bookstore's appeal "is less loud, more profound, less distinct, more stirring—and sooner forgotten. Yet its effect endures for ever."[17]

The rhythm of the bookstore is conducive to what Calvino calls "the spaciousness of humanistic leisure."[18] To accommodate this spaciousness, there must be some constriction or emptying of our concerns. Many a browser, by virtue of browsing, creates mental capacity where there had been none. The sort of focus required of the browser also facilitates a quieting of obstreperous emotions and thoughts; anxiety, self-satisfaction, regret, and insecurity, for instance, are exposed as ephemeral and overwhelmingly illusory.

The browser is both in and out of their own head, both in and out of another's head. The lion, as Valéry says, is made of assimilated sheep.[19] Calvino, we'll recall, speaks to this question of identity, asking who we are "if not a combinatoria of experiences, information, books we have read, things imagined."[20] The browser's mind thinks others' thoughts, and, after rumination and digestion, others' thoughts become the browser's.

The bookstore, then, to return to Conrad's artist,

speaks to our capacity for delight and wonder, to the sense of mystery surrounding our lives; to our sense of pity, and beauty, and pain; to the latent feeling of fellowship with all creation—and to the subtle but invincible conviction of solidarity that knits together the loneliness of innumerable hearts, to the solidarity in dreams, in joy, in sorrow, in aspirations, in illusions, in hope, in fear, which binds men to each other, which binds together all humanity—the dead to the living and the living to the unborn.[21]

Unprotected, in the solitude of another's thought, with a certain inner hygiene, we find ourselves capable of taking the time to listen to one another, to listen to ourselves. We are ready to receive whatever blessings the bookstore has to offer.

ARS RUMINATIVA

There are adjacencies in time, as there are in space; in the good bookstore, we are, again, coeval with our finest writers. We move amid not just the peaks of our age, but also, as Musil eulogized Rilke, "the pinnacles on which the destiny of the spirit strides across ages."[22]

The bookstore compresses time, taking us to a dimension where the ancient languages are once again spoken; the Awadhi songs of the Ramayana are sung, the theories of the Amoraim are unfolded patiently, Ibn Rushd reflects upon the complete works of Aristotle, and the soliloquies of Shakespeare move us as though we are hearing them for the first time. And the books of Anne Carson and Leon Forrest and Eliot Weinberger and Preti Taneja, written with the wisdom of the ancients, beckon.

Time dilates as we browse.

• • •

Calvino observed that "in every text he writes, in any way he can, Borges manages to talk about the infinite, the uncountable, time, eternity or rather the eternal presence or cyclical nature of time."[23] In his story "The Garden of Forking Paths," Borges creates more suspense through his meditations on time than through his brilliant plotting of a murder. The narrator reads an account of Dr. Yu Tsun, who believes that his forebear Ts'ui Pên's "inviolate and perfect" construction was both a labyrinth and a book. He knows it was infinite and struggles to comprehend its ontology. He imagines it as "a labyrinth of labyrinths, of one sinuous spreading labyrinth that would encompass the past and the future and in some way involve the stars," and recognizes that the garden's paths fork in time, not space. Yu is told that Ts'ui "believed in an infinite series of times, in a growing, dizzying net of divergent, convergent, and parallel times. This network of times which approached one another, forked, broke off, or were unaware of one another for centuries, embraces *all* possibilities of time."[24]

Borges and I imagine the garden of forking paths not just as a book but also as a library or a bookstore.

Perhaps the bookstore, like the library, is the storehouse of memory—what Carlyle called "the articulate audible voice of the Past, when the body and material substance of it has altogether vanished like a dream."[25] For centuries, before printing, remembering was a vital and critical human activity. "The making of this inventory," the medievalist Mary Carruthers explains, "was considered to be in itself an art—the craft of memory, *ars memorativa*. Recollection was a type of investigation, of discovery and invention."[26]

We can see why Stumm felt as though he were walking through an enormous brain in that state library. And perhaps some ancient part of him, some ancient part of us, responds to the space accordingly. The good bookstore, with its diagrammed sections containing a collection of humanity's inquiry and imagination, reflection and exploration, serves as an aid to memory, yes, but to reflection and rumination as well. And so the *ars memorativa* of the ancients, that constructed theater of the mind, diagrammed in order to develop logically consistent, if idiosyncratic, systems for memorizing vast works, has become the *ars ruminativa* of the browsing memorious ones, the ruminating slow ones, who walk these physical diagrams—Borgesian labyrinths—with chronometers that measure time across the ages, ruminating as a type of investigation, of discovery, of invention.

The art of rumination brings us out of ourselves and our time. It quiets the ephemeral concerns we carried across the threshold of the shop. If we create these storehouses of ruminants, we might develop a perpetual din composed of thoughts and insights that endure. They persist, as Calvino writes, "as a background noise even when the most incompatible momentary concerns are in control of the situation."[27] These children of their time and begetters of ages, these books of the hour and books of all time, became our constant companions. These static texts become dynamic as our identities develop, and they become aids to ruminations, that we might better acquaint ourselves with ourselves and with our world.

● ● ●

A declaration made by the poet and scholar Eve Ewing in 2017, at an event in our stores, resounds. "Now, more than ever," she said, "I am sick of people saying, 'Now, more than ever.'"

How do we understand the distinction between *now* and *ever*? While the promise of something new might goad us to read the next article or watch the next episode, it is by connecting ourselves to that which endures—the classic that persists as background noise—that we may understand the concerns of the moment. By saying, "Now *as* ever," by looking not to the next new thing but to the last enduring thing, we are more likely to grasp our unique and not so unique challenges, to learn the origin of a particular narrative, perhaps to subvert that narrative, to attempt to find meaning after tragedy, or to comprehend the capacity, complexity, and diversity of human nature, experience, and knowledge.

At its best, the serious bookstore inspires this engagement. It strives to create a space that values slow time. It privileges attention above sensation, recognition above seduction. And it privileges good books of the moment and of all time by children of their time as well as begetters of ages. And finally, it privileges records and expressions of the enduring and ephemeral that are worthy of encounter.

In his essay "Experience," written after he suffered great personal loss, Emerson wonders:

> If any of us knew what we were doing, or where we are going, then when we think we best know! We do not know today whether we are busy or idle. In times when we thought ourselves indolent, we have afterwards discovered that much was accomplished, and much was begun in us. All our days are so unprofitable while they pass, that 'tis wonderful where or when we ever got anything of this which we call wisdom, poetry, virtue. We never got it on any dated calendar day. Some heavenly days must have been intercalated somewhere.[28]

Browsers revel in this intercalated time. These moments are expansive; they are, somehow, not at the mercy of the clock. Here, the only urgency is the one created by the books themselves; the stacks are stuffed with them. Read one of those Lispector novels—she'll tell you "of the instants that drip and are thick with blood."[29] Browse the classics section—you'll know with Heraclitus that "time is a child playing draughts."[30] Pursue that bookseller's lead and you'll hear from Weil how, "in the inner life, time takes the place of space."[31] Perhaps you will reflect upon your own capacity for thought. Pick up one of those translations of *Confessions*—perhaps Sarah Ruden's—and reflect upon the unfathomable repository of time: "In you, my mind, I measure time. Don't shout me down with the protest that time is a thing in itself. Don't shout yourself down with a riot of your feelings. In you, I say, I measure time."[32] And further down the page, you'll measure, along with Augustine, the silence.

AN INTERLUDE:
FROM "LE MONOCLE DE MON ONCLE"

IV.

This luscious and impeccable fruit of life
Falls, it appears, of its own weight to earth.

An apple serves as well as any skull
To be the book in which to read a round,
And is as excellent, in that it is composed

Of what, like skulls, comes rotting back to ground.
But it excels in this, that as the fruit
Of love, it is a book too mad to read
Before one merely reads to pass the time.

V.

In the high west there burns a furious star.

The measure of the intensity of love
Is measure, also, of the verve of earth.
For me, the firefly's quick, electric stroke
Ticks tediously the time of one more year.

VIII.

It comes, it blooms, it bears its fruit and dies.
This trivial trope reveals a way of truth.
Our bloom is gone. We are the fruit thereof.[33]

• • •

Stars and blossoming fruit trees: utter permanence and extreme fragility give one an equal sense of eternity.[34]

THE DURATION OF TWILIGHT

The Talmud begins with an argument about time. The sages are discussing the measure of the period during which one is allowed to say the evening

Shema prayer. They proceed with a series of attempts to define "twilight."

The metaphors and measurements abound. Nehemiah thinks twilight lasts "as long as it takes a man to walk half a *mil.*" Hanina tries to further illuminate the measurement, commenting that those who wish to know the length of Nehemiah's twilight "should leave Carmel's summit while the sun is still shining, go down and take a dip in the sea, and come up again."

Yose: "Twilight is like the twinkling of an eye as night enters and the day departs, and it is impossible to determine its length."

Judah: "How long does twilight last? After sunset, as long as the east still has a reddish glow; when the lower [sky] is pale but not the upper, it is twilight; [but] when the upper [sky] is as pale as the lower, it is night."

Meir prefers Yose's standard for measuring the duration of twilight to Judah's and he tells Judah as much. I prefer Tanhuma's: "To what may twilight be compared?" he asks. "To a drop of blood placed on the tip of a sword—the instant it takes the drop to divide into two parts, that is twilight."[35]

• • •

Later, in the tractate *Pesachim*, the sages identify the last of God's creations: the ten phenomena created at twilight on the first Sabbath eve. Sabbath eve is the moment that cleaves the holy and the worldly. That is, the moment both distinguishes and binds the holy and the worldly, as twilight binds night and day. What is created in this moment is created with all of these elements.

In the good company of other magical creations like Miriam's well,* which provided water to the wandering Jews in the desert, manna, which provided them food, and the rainbow, which represented God's promise to not destroy the world by flood,† several tools of clarification were created at twilight on Sabbath eve: writing, the writing instrument, and the tablets.

•   •   •

Night drags on, And I am sated with tossings till morning twilight.

—JOB 7:4

THE DURATION OF DAWN

The instant that is thick and drips with blood. The instant it takes one drop to become two. That instant is the duration of all instants, no matter how dilated

---

* "One who wants to see Miriam's well, which accompanied the Jewish people throughout their sojourn in the desert, should do the following: He should climb to the top of Mount Carmel and look out [at the Mediterranean Sea], and he will see a rock that looks like a sieve in the sea, and that is Miriam's Well" (Shabbat, 35a). And we know from Nehemiah that the descent and a dip in the sea lasts the duration of twilight.

† "Yea, foolish mortals, Noah's flood is not yet subsided; two thirds of the fair world it yet covers" (Melville, *Moby-Dick*, 298–99).

or contracted, and it is the duration of the present moment—the only time we inhabit, the time in which all things occur. Borges reflected "that everything happens to a man precisely, precisely *now*. Centuries of centuries and only in the present do things happen."[36] As a receptacle, it is indifferent. Bachelard thinks that, "if our heart were large enough to love life in all its detail," we would see every instant as both giver and plunderer.[37] We must maintain vigilance against the plunder.

· · ·

The poet Paul Valéry's notebooks were composed during an hour of uncertainty, an hour suitable to the exploration of uncertainty. "I have a habit," he writes, with his singular elegance, "the moment I get up, before the dawn, in that pure and pregnant hour of daybreak, midway between lamplight and sunlight, of jotting down all that comes into my mind, unsummoned."[38]

The notebooks abound with explorations of time. He asks the question "What is a moment?" and answers it with questions: "Something instantaneous as a lightning flash? Or is it something that, however multiplied, could not compose a period of time; the *contrary* of a period of time, not an element of it?"[39] And elsewhere,

The past astonishes the present.
The work of years astounds the moment.[40]

Quignard thinks that we might prefer the more certain word "passing" to the word "present," acknowledging that every moment is experienced as fleeting. But not all moments feel the same, of course, fleeting though they may be. Some feel fulfilling, some strike us as wasted. Some last too long—they seem interminable—and some feel so fleeting—how we wish we could arrest the flow of time! How can we decelerate the moment that we might observe the tip of an autumn hair? "Sometimes," Hyde thinks, "then, if we are awake, if the artist really was gifted, the work will induce a moment of grace, a communion, a period during which we too know the hidden coherence of our being and feel the fullness of our lives."[41] Can we create the conditions that put readers in touch with the concentrate of knowledge?

Whether by remembering the reverie induced by a line of poetry or a certain felicitous turn of phrase; whether by retracing the paths on which we discovered the ideas we hold dear, or saw others in our community engaging a book we love, or a book we expect to, knowing this bookstore is ours alone *and* unowned simultaneously; whether by knowing that the conditions created by the booksellers provide reliable grounds of rumination that tacitly urge a more expansive perspective on whatever vexation arises; whether by seeking that one book that will meet this given moment in precisely the way we need, even if the moment is not shareable with others—nor shareable with our future selves even—and knowing that we have mastered the art of browsing in bookstores, confident that our pickaxes and shovels will serve us as we need; perhaps, on occasion, we will experience, by dint of this rumination we've honed on the pleasure grounds of our bookstores, what Bachelard calls "the sudden inflection of human genius upon the curvature of life's progress," a moment, he writes, "when knowledge, by shedding light on passion, detects at once the rules and relentlessness of destiny."[42]

I am one of many who, in the corners and crevices of the bookstore, have stilled, "for the space of the breath," as Conrad said, "the hands busy about the work of the earth." I have become "entranced by the sight of distant goals to glance for a moment at the surrounding vision of form and color, of sunshine and shadows." "Behold!" Conrad continues, "all the truth of life is there: a moment of vision, a sigh, a smile—and the return to an eternal rest."[43]

Joseph Joubert, the sublime aphorist, had a bit of the *sandpiper* in him when he said, "In a moment of insight you can perceive everything; but it takes years for exactitude to give it expression."[44] These are the measures destined for our souls, these the moments intercalated. Lispector knows that "the instant is this one. The instant is of an imminence that takes my breath away. The instant is in itself imminent. At the same time that I live it, I burst into its passage into another instant."[45]

Robinson speaks of "a compounding of time, so that we can see how things tend, and how they might complete themselves out of the constrained variables of the reality we posit for them."[46] On a similar tip, Valéry notes that "the 'future' is the most perceptible fraction of the present moment."[47] One moment is a succession of moments. And, as Whitman says, "time is ample."[48] The instant, like twilight containing both day and night, contains the past and the future.

UNCERTAINTY

The most precious thing in life is uncertainty.
—KENKŌ, *Essays in Idleness*, 7

Twilight itself is a period of uncertainty. Its length, as we have discussed, is uncertain, but so is its nature. The sages discussed the range of implications of the ambiguity of twilight. "It is uncertain whether it consists of both day and night, it is uncertain whether it is completely day, and it is uncertain whether it is completely night."[49] It's not a coincidence that clarifying tools were created during the last hour of worldly time, in an ambiguous moment, before the beginning of the first Sabbath, the first sacred hour. Only tools born of uncertainty will help us see clearly.

Within the context of the discussion around twilight, the sages discussed the unknowable. Try as we might to understand certain phenomena, their uncertainty will persist, as they are not given to us to know, yet our inquiry persists. What, at last, is the point of the bookseller's work—the filtration, selection, assemblage, and enthusiasm? What is that something, something, something for which we readers are looking? Is it possible that we know that which we seek to be ultimately unknowable? Undiscoverable? And yet we seek anyway, if only to tighten the circumference around the inquiry.*

The sages taught that seven matters are concealed from us:

1. The time of death
2. The time of consolation
3. The profundity of justice
4. What is in the heart of another
5. In what way we might fulfill our calling
6. The restoration of the reign of loving-kindness
7. The obliteration of the wicked[50]

• • •

"Why are we reading," asks Dillard,

if not in the hope of beauty laid bare, life heightened and its deepest mystery probed? . . . Why are we reading if not in hope that the writer will magnify and dramatize our days, will illuminate and inspire us with wisdom, courage, and the possibility of meaningfulness, and will press upon our

---

* To paraphrase Rabbi Tarfon (Pirkei Avos 2:21): it is not incumbent upon us to answer the question, nor are we free to abandon the inquiry.

minds the deepest mysteries, so we may feel again their majesty and power?[51]

Perhaps it is all about encountering uncertainty, confronting the majestic and powerful mysteries, not giving up hope that the concealed will be revealed, that uncertainties will clarify, but knowing that, even if they never do—and they likely never will—we will dwell in these moments all the same, even if for only the instant when one drop of blood on the tip of a sword becomes two.

THE BOOKSELLER'S CREDO

Of such moments, she thought, the thing is made that endures.
—VIRGINIA WOOLF, *To the Lighthouse*, 107

Once we have entered slow or immersive time, we are more receptive to the memory and imaginings of humanity. Our instant is more generous—more giver than plunderer. The current of time relents when we browse. The bookseller's task might better be rendered in light of this phenomenon. Conrad wonders whether the artist might play a role in bringing these moments of slow time the gravity of which they, and we, are worthy. And here I find something of the bookseller's credo.

If, like Whitman, we do not convince by argument, simile, or rhyme, but convince by our presence, how might we provide an answer to those who have exhausted the appeal of the ephemeral and are no longer looking for immediate satisfaction or vacuous stimulation? What do we say to those who, as Conrad indicates, demand to be consoled or amused, "who demand to be promptly improved, or encouraged, or frightened, or shocked, or charmed"? The aspiration of the bookseller is to provide the conditions, by the power of the good bookstore, to slow the reader down that they might behold a more capacious vision of the possible. If we succeed, like Conrad's artist, the reader will find there, according to their desserts, "encouragement, consolation, fear, charm." They will find all that they demand, and perhaps also "that glimpse of truth" for which they have forgotten to ask.[52]

That glimpse, snatched "in a moment of courage, from the remorseless rush of time," when encountered deliberately, with sincerity and tenderness, "might reveal the substance of its truth—disclose its inspiring secret: the stress and passion within the core of each convincing moment." Conrad concludes that

the presented vision of regret or pity, of terror or mirth, shall awaken in the hearts of the beholders that feeling of unavoidable solidarity; of the solidarity in mysterious origin, in toil, in joy, in hope, in uncertain fate, which binds men to each other and all mankind to the visible world.[53]

And so might we be bound. My hope is that we, this society struggling to be born, will recall the most important debts—those debts beyond the currency of the banks and financiers—and acquit ourselves of them by building models and systems that allow the gifts we have received, and those we create, to subsequently pass to the next generation. Let us commit to preserving and tending the gardens required to patiently cultivate these receptacles of meaning, the concentrate of knowledge, these talismans of possibility. They are ours to create, if we want them.

The Good Bookstore

AN EPILOGUE

A bookstore is always found on the edge of a grand
avenue that leads nowhere but from book to book,
delivered over to itself and following the tracks of its idea,
word for word indefinitely reprinted, a grand avenue
along which this emotional and subtle commerce of
thinking never ceases.

—JEAN-LUC NANCY, *On the Commerce of Thinking*, 45

After the legendary Parisian bookshop La Hune shut
its doors in 2015, Adam Gopnik lamented, "When a
bookstore closes, an argument ends."[1] In the spring
of 2020, we experienced the silence; the argument,
miraculously, merely paused.

For nearly sixty years, in times of uncertainty, our
community has descended upon the bookstore, looking for camaraderie, meaning, and provisions for the
journey, as they tried to understand ruptures, both
global and personal. The rupture of March 2020 was
different. The pull of the place itself suddenly seemed
like a danger, not a salve, to our community. The
density of the crowd was not comforting, as it had
been in the past—it was terrifying. For the first time
in our history, and for the next 441 days, the doors of

both the Seminary Co-op and 57th Street Books were closed for an extended period.*

During the closure, these bookstores, bereft of their community indefinitely, were not indifferent spaces, to use Bachelard's term. They weren't subject to the measures and estimates of the surveyor. They were haunted spaces, thick with ghosts. While the booksellers worked in the stores, among books, during the entirety of the COVID-19 pandemic—even during the frenetic and terrifying spring season—we found ourselves operating a warehouse fulfillment center, not a bookstore. It might seem obvious to note that there is a significant difference between the two, but considering the fact that our industry is now built to support warehouse fulfillment centers, not bookstores, it's important to clearly mark the difference.

Bookstores are roused by their patrons; it is the encounter that fulfills a bookstore's purpose. Reopening the doors in June 2021 felt like a resuscitation first, then a revival. If an argument ends when a bookstore closes, what argument is continued when a bookstore remains open?

•   •   •

According to Ilan Stavans, the scholar of Latin American literature and publisher of Restless Books, Borges so identified with the culture of Judaism that

---

* The store was closed for nine days in 2012 when the collection was moved from the basement of the Seminary to its current location.

he rigorously sought a genealogical connection to the Jewish people, to no avail. "In response," Stavans writes, "he simply imagined himself a Jew."[2] What was it about the culture of the Jews that created such an affinity in Borges?

The Jews are a people who are raised to question—interrogate even—their god. They do so through commentary primarily, not criticism. Their libraries (like my grandfather's), composed of volumes of loving expansion of their canon, might be all they'll ever know as home. After all, they are fated to wander—a rootless people who are perennial strangers in strange lands. Without a homeland, the Jewish people made of the book their homeland.

Borges was a reader first. As Hardwick notes, for Borges "the library is the landscape of human drama; it is experience, tragedy, social history."[3] As Jews made of their homeland a book, so Borges and I made of the library and the bookstore, respectively, a homeland. And perhaps the imagined book that might best represent our homeland, as the Talmud represents the homeland of Jews, is the catalog of catalogs.

Like all people of the book, Borges was in search of the catalog of catalogs. We booksellers compile our own versions of the catalog of catalogs. We fancy ourselves their authors—or, perhaps, their editors—and create our editions, with annual supplements, withdrawals, errata, and some revisions.

When I first visited Cella's catalog of catalogs, the 1994 edition of the Seminary Co-op, I was ineluctably persuaded of the necessity of the Seminary Co-op by the fact of its existence. Like the members of the Cartographers Guild who, as Borges wrote in his exceedingly short story "On Exactitude in Science," struck a "Map of the Empire whose size was that of the Empire, and which coincided point for point with it," Cella, Yamazaki, Jones, McNally, and their ilk created their bookstore-shaped catalogs year after year.[4] The catalog is unabridged.* Its geography can only be mapped point for point.

In some way, we are all wandering people, wandering in search of our communities, in search of ourselves. Books and the landscapes they create, both as objects and as mechanisms to deliver the hopes, dreams, moods, principles, and wisdom contained between their covers, are exceptional tools to cultivate our own interior landscape, which, after all, is our portable and permanent homeland. And so we may understand, shape, and immerse ourselves in the external world, creating what Robinson calls a sense of the possible, that we might become a more generous community.[5]

• • •

This book is no eulogy. We can't allow that. It is a celebration and a hope that the argument of the Seminary Co-op and its institutional kin—bookstores that create an unalloyed bookish space—will flourish for generations to come. And so, rather than

* "You can't abridge a melody" (Valéry, *Analects,* 213).

provide general answers, I hope to provoke questions that individuals and communities might consider as they develop their own arguments, that is, their own bookstores.

How might we learn to use bookstores? How might we develop more than an inkling of what "one of the greatest instruments" can accomplish?

How might we accurately assess the value provided by good bookstores—those that patiently carry a mix of books of the moment and books of all time?

How might we look to good bookstores to help provide a bookish landscape that supports conversation, contemplation, and the development of a more learned (as opposed to educated or degreed) populace?

How might we establish the profession of bookselling that we might develop careers and offer proper remuneration for those readers of reading without whom good bookstores couldn't exist?

How might we deliberately build a financial model for good bookstores, rather than try to fit them into an inherited retail mold? Our model must recognize that the product is not the book itself, but the experience of the bookstore—its browsage, and the thoughts, conversations, and discoveries the collection evokes.

• • •

Like Borges, I am a reader first, which also means I'm one of the quiet, bookish thousands who ruminate during a good browse. As much as I have written from the perspective of a career bookseller, it is as a bookstore enthusiast that I file these dispatches. I steward the Seminary Co-op because I want to live in a world with bookstores like the Seminary Co-op. It's a selfish endeavor, really—or it would be if I thought I was the only one (we are legion, we thousands)—but that is the truth of the matter. These bookish landscapes built me as I built them.

I hope, like the Good Life or the Good Society, that the Good Bookstore can serve as our ambition. There is something distinctive about the good bookstore, the loss of which would lead to a loss of a particular way of being in the world.

ACKNOWLEDGMENTS

Books are created by so many, despite the lone name printed on the spine. While I can't repay the most important debts I have incurred, I can certainly acknowledge them with profound gratitude.

I am indebted to countless booksellers with whom I have served over the years. Some whose conversations, support, and camaraderie were particularly important in conceiving of and writing this book include Kasia Bartoszynska, Franny Billingsley, Caroline Casey, Kaitlynn Cassady, Sonja Coates, Joy Dallanegra-Sanger, Stephanie Denton, Stéphanie D'Hubert, Clancey D'Isa, John Evans, BrocheAroe Fabian, Rebecca Fitting, Allison Hill, Kim Hooyboer, Alex Houston, Brad Jonas, Alena Jones, Janet Jones, Elizabeth Jordan, Elaine Katzenberger, Greg Kornbluh, Freddie Lippmann, Bryce Lucas, April Lundberg, Jenny Macagba, Praveen Madan, Marina Malzoniya, Walter Martin, Vanessa Martini, Colin McDonald, Sarah McNally, Lynn Mooney, Christine Onorati, Melinda Powers, Alison Reid, Shuchi Saraswat, Thulasi Seshan, Cliff Simms, Rick Simonson, Oren Teicher, Alyson Turner, Stephanie Valdez, Dorothea von Moltke, Jonathon Welch, and Lisa Winn.

I have been inspired by scores of colleagues in publishing, including Ellen Adler, Elise Cannon, Jennifer Crewe, John Donatich, Susan Donnelly, John Eklund, Morgan Entrekin, Barbara Epler, Alan Harvey, Brad Hebel, Judy Hottensen, Leslie Jobson, John Kessler, Garrett Kiely, Ruth Liebmann, Lara Phan, Michael Reynolds, Sharmila Sen, Alan Thomas, David Underwood, and Diane Wachtell.

I would have been lost without early career mentors such as Devra Siegel, Carol VanderVeen, and Jay Zalewski.

I have received warm and wise support and friendship from Deborah Epstein, Ken Warren, and Katie Parsons, as well as Erin Adams, Stuart Flack, Julie Getzels, Melina Hale, Philip Halpern, Mark Hansen, William G. Howell, Mike Levine, Natalie Moore, Nicholas Pearce, Julie Peterson, Darren Reisberg, Martha Roth, James Schwinn, DeWitt Scott, Bill Sewell, Douglas Sharps, Jack Spicer, Connie Spreen, Stephen Stigler, and Hal Wilde.

The care and conversation of good friends is beyond measure. There are too many to name, but this book could not exist without the dialogues with dear friends and fellow travelers Jeff Bartow, Lori Berko, Jon Bibo, Jessica Biggs, T. David Brent, Ada Calhoun, Arianna Cisneros, Duane Davis, Wendy Doniger, Elizabeth Branch Dyson, Eve L. Ewing, Sunny Fisher, Wes Freeman, Joanie Friedman, Sam Gee, Kimiko Guthrie, Khari Humphries, Parneshia Jones, Jamie Kalven, Carrie Kiryakakis, Greg Kiryakakis, Naveen Kishore, Manya Lempert, Ashley McCullough, Priya

Nelson, Peter Nilson, Ydalmi Noriega, Hilesh Patel, Mike Rodriguez, Dawn Rogers, Debra Shaffer Seaman, Donna Seaman, Sadia Sindhu, Michael Skeer, Adam Sonderberg, Meghan Sullivan, Preti Taneja, Susana Vasquez, Freddie Washington, and Ian West.

Alberto Manguel and Paul Yamazaki have led the way. I hope to honor their influence.

The staff of Princeton University Press is wonderful. I am grateful to Kate Farquhar-Thomson, Chris Ferrante, Sara Lerner, Erin Suydam, and Maria Whelan for creating and supporting this book.

I have adapted some material from my annual letters to the Seminary Co-op community. I am indebted to those who read early drafts of the annual letters and, especially, the manuscript. Their generosity with their time, criticisms, and shared passion for the project helped make the book significantly better. Thank you, Kasia Bartoszynska, Clancey D'Isa, Christie Henry, Alena Jones, Manya Lempert, Alberto Manguel, Priya Nelson, Peter Nilson, Leah Price, Adam Sonderberg, and Paul Yamazaki.

I am grateful to the peer reviewers whose critiques and enthusiasms helped improve the manuscript at a critical juncture. A few editors helped improve the sense and style of the book. Cynthia Buck's copyedits were thoughtful and elegant. Matt Rohal is an extraordinary editor and was instrumental in finetuning the manuscript. Rob Tempio is one of the best in the business. I am grateful for his sensibility, joyfulness, and passion for great books and good bookstores. This book wouldn't exist without his vision.

ACKNOWLEDGMENTS

Special thanks to Jack Cella, Katy O'Brien-Weintraub, Richard Barnard, Rodney Powell, Heather Ahrenholz, and the volumes of booksellers who built the Seminary Co-op and 57ᵗʰ Street Books. And to Art Sussman, who, in telling me that the palm trees at Stanford weren't real, convinced me that I needed to come to Chicago to steward the Seminary Co-op Bookstore.

We lost Sandy Ackerman, Sonny Mehta, Marshall Sahlins, Michael Seidenberg, and Judy Zitske as this book was being written. All five of them made a difference. The legacies of Sol Deutsch and John Paul Yen are a constant presence.

I can't overstate the profound influence that Harry Davis, Hanna Gray, and Christie Henry have had on me. Finding paragons this late in life is a privilege I don't take for granted.

I'm grateful to my loving family, who have been there from the beginning: to Erica, Haskell, and Linda; to the next generation: Coby, and Willow, Wyatt, and Waylon; and to those whose familial bond is no less meaningful for being a bit younger: Susan, David, Danielle, Jen, Chris, Laura, Brandon, Brooke, and Nikke.

May, becoming I, I say "you."

THE PRESENCE OF BOOKS: AN INTRODUCTION

1. Shils, "The Bookstore in America," 102.
2. *The Booksellers' League*, 33–34.
3. Nancy, "Bookseller."
4. Kawaguchi, "Feminist Feast and Famine."
5. Nawotka, "ABA Added 111 Stores in 2019."
6. Shils, "The Bookstore in America," 95.
7. Mencken, "Lo, the Poor Bookseller."
8. Morley, *John Mistletoe*, 286.
9. Shils, "The Bookstore in America," 103.
10. Grothaus, "A Rediscovered 1997 Video Reveals Why Jeff Bezos Chose Books."
11. These excerpts are drawn from the Seminary Co-op's articles of incorporation, dated October 18, 1961.
12. Shils, "The Bookstore in America," 98.
13. Quoted in Doherty and Kwong, *If You Weren't Looking for It*, 53.
14. Hunt, "My Books," in Hunt, *The World of Books and Other Essays*, 17.
15. Lamb, "Oxford in the Vacation," in Lamb, *The Essays of Elia*, 12.
16. Bacon, *Of the Proficience and Advancement of Learning*, 90.
17. Weil, *Gravity and Grace*, 161.
18. Burton, *The Anatomy of Melancholy*, 457–58.
19. *The Booksellers' League*, 36.
20. Shils, "The Bookstore in America," 98.
21. Nancy, *On the Commerce of Thinking*, 36–37.
22. Shils, "The Bookstore in America," 93.
23. Whitman, "Song of the Open Road, 10," in Whitman, *Poetry and Prose*, 303.

CHAPTER ONE. SPACE

1. Bachelard, *The Poetics of Space*, 19.
2. UChicago Architecture, "Stanley Tigerman on the Seminary Co-op Bookstore."
3. Kalven, "Browsing in the Labyrinth."
4. Cappello, *Lecture*, 115.
5. Ibid., 39.
6. Liu, *The Huainanzi*, 50.
7. Montaigne, "Of Three Kinds of Association," in *The Complete Essays of Montaigne*, 629.
8. Kenkō, *Essays in Idleness*, 16.
9. Ibid., 7.
10. Ibid., 70–71.
11. Carter, "Introduction," in Carter, ed., *The Columbia Anthology of Japanese Essays*, 2.
12. Lowell, *Among My Books*, 9–10.
13. Ibid., 314.
14. Locke, *Of the Conduct of the Understanding*, in *The Educational Writings of John Locke*, 216–17.
15. Morley, *John Mistletoe*, 66.
16. Jackson, *The Anatomy of Bibliomania*, 55.
17. Laertius, *Lives of Eminent Philosophers*, 445–47.
18. Barnes, *The Complete Works of Aristotle*, 1825.
19. Epicurus, *The Essential Epicurus*, 85.
20. Seneca, *Epistulae Morales*, 147.
21. Bachelard, *The Poetics of Space*, 19.
22. Manguel, *A History of Reading*, 193.
23. Quoted in Doherty and Kwong, *If You Weren't Looking for It*, 27.
24. Ruskin, *Sesame and Lilies*, 34.
25. Ibid., 35.
26. Hippocrates, *Hippocrates*, vol. IV, 473.
27. Walpole, *Correspondence*, 26:307–8, reprinted in Silver, "The Prehistory of Serendipity, from Bacon to Walpole."
28. Silver, "The Prehistory of Serendipity," 237.
29. Ruskin, *Sesame and Lilies*, 34.
30. Musil, *The Man without Qualities*, 115.
31. Robinson, *When I Was a Child I Read Books*, 22–23.
32. Perec, "Brief Notes on the Art and Manner of Arranging One's Books," in Perec, *Species of Spaces and Other Pieces*, 150.

33. Stevens, "Man Carrying Thing," in Stevens, *Collected Poetry and Prose*, 306.
34. Manguel, *A History of Reading*, 187.
35. Schonwald, "The Seminary Co-op Turns Another Page."
36. Perec, "Brief Notes on the Art and Manner of Arranging One's Books," in Perec, *Species of Spaces and Other Pieces*, 155.
37. Ibid., 152–53.
38. Battles, *Library*, 106.
39. Jirō, "A Bed for My Books," in Carter, ed., *The Columbia Anthology of Japanese Essays*, 457.
40. Laertius, *Lives of Eminent Philosophers*, 465–75.
41. Weinberger, *The Ghosts of Birds*, 195–203.
42. Gupta, "A Bookstore with a Difference."
43. Borges, "Fragments of an Apocryphal Gospel," in Borges, *Selected Poems*, 295.
44. Manguel, *A History of Reading*, 198.
45. Ibid., 199.
46. UChicago Architecture, "Stanley Tigerman on the Seminary Co-op Bookstore."
47. Alena Jones, correspondence with the author, May 2018.
48. Ibid.
49. Schenden, "Entering the Thin Places."
50. Thoreau, *Walden and Civil Disobedience*, 181.
51. Nicholson Baker, correspondence with the author, September 9, 2016.

CHAPTER TWO. ABUNDANCE

1. Ranganathan, *The Five Laws of Library Science*.
2. Manguel, *Packing My Library*, 99.
3. Calvino, *The Uses of Literature*, 81.
4. Musil, *The Man without Qualities*, 500.
5. Ibid., 500–501.
6. Ibid., 501.
7. Bialik and Ravnitzky, *The Book of Legends*, 422.
8. Morley, *John Mistletoe*, 158.
9. Quoted in London Library, *On Reading, Writing, and Living with Books*, 86.
10. Lamb, "Detached Thoughts on Books and Reading," in Lamb, *The Essays of Elia*, 195.

11. Hunt, "My Books," in Hunt, *The World of Books and Other Essays*, 33.
12. Quoted in Richardson, *First We Read, Then We Write*, 9.
13. Quoted in Doherty and Kwong, *If You Weren't Looking for It*, 53.
14. O'Brien, *The Browser's Ecstasy*, 33.
15. Calvino, *Six Memos for the Next Millennium*, 116.
16. Quignard, *The Roving Shadows*, 77.
17. Liu, *The Huainanzi*, 631.
18. Blake, "The Marriage of Heaven and Hell," in Blake, *The Complete Poetry and Prose of William Blake*, 38.
19. Bishop, "Sandpiper," in Bishop, *Poems*, 129.
20. Melville, *Moby-Dick, or, The Whale*, 298–99.
21. Ibid., 230.
22. Ibid., 597.
23. Musil, *The Man without Qualities*, 405.
24. Ibid., 500–501.
25. Emerson, "Books," in Emerson, *Society and Solitude*, 185.
26. Zaid, *So Many Books*, 22.
27. Borges et al., "Poetry: Jorge Luis Borges," 111.
28. Jewett, *The Facts and Considerations Relative to the Duties on Books*, 22.
29. McColvin, *How to Use Books*, 10.
30. Zaid, *So Many Books*, 21.
31. Macaulay, *Personal Pleasures*.
32. Pound, *ABC of Reading*, 17.
33. Emerson, "Books," in Emerson, *Society and Solitude*, 183.
34. Quoted in Doherty and Kwong, *If You Weren't Looking for It*, 52.
35. Borges, "The Library of Babel," in Borges, *Labyrinths*, 52.
36. Musil, *The Man without Qualities*, 502.
37. Ibid.
38. O'Brien, *The Browser's Ecstasy*, 35.
39. Borges, "The Library of Babel," in Borges, *Labyrinths*, 53.
40. Quoted in Manguel, *Packing My Library*, 15.
41. Lessing, *The Golden Notebook*, xii.
42. Woolf, "The Novels of George Meredith," in Woolf, *The Second Common Reader*, 234.
43. Canetti, *The Agony of Flies*, 231 (emphasis in original).
44. Calvino, *The Uses of Literature*, 133.
45. Quoted in Zaid, *So Many Books*, 12.
46. Sontag, *As Consciousness Is Harnessed to Flesh*, 510.
47. Zaid, *So Many Books*, 33.

48. Quoted in Doherty and Kwong, *If You Weren't Looking for It*, 28.
49. Calvino, *Six Memos for the Next Millennium*, 124.

CHAPTER THREE. VALUE

1. De Bury, *The Philobiblon*, 17.
2. Ibid.
3. Quoted in Ordine, *The Usefulness of the Useless*, 101.
4. Quoted in London Library, *On Reading, Writing and Living with Books*, 89.
5. Okakura, *The Book of Tea*, 85.
6. Quoted in Doherty and Kwong, *If You Weren't Looking for It*, 27.
7. McColvin, *How to Use Books*, 50.
8. Ordine, *The Usefulness of the Useless*, 5.
9. Quoted in ibid., 4.
10. Quoted in ibid., 82.
11. Quoted in ibid., 54–55.
12. Gissing, *The Private Papers of Henry Ryecroft*, 37.
13. Quoted in Quignard, *The Roving Shadows*, 123.
14. St. Jerome quoted in Leonard, *The Booklovers' Anthology*, 248; Quignard, *The Roving Shadows*, 120.
15. Hyde, *The Gift*, 60.
16. Whitman, "Song of the Open Road," *Poetry and Prose*, 300.
17. Hyde, *The Gift*, xii.
18. Ruskin, "Unto This Last," in Ruskin, *Unto This Last and Other Writings*, 161.
19. Gandhi, *An Autobiography*, 90.
20. Ibid., 299.
21. Ruskin, "Unto This Last," in Ruskin, *Unto This Last and Other Writings*, 178.
22. Ibid., 176.
23. Ibid., 178.
24. Ibid.
25. Ibid., 173.
26. Ibid., 174.
27. Ibid., 187.
28. Hyde, *The Gift*, xii.
29. Ibid., 107.
30. De Bury, *The Philobiblon*, 17.

31. Quoted in Cole, *Responsibilities of the American Book Community*, 44.
32. Quoted in ibid., 44.
33. Quoted in ibid., 18 (emphasis added).
34. Morley, *John Mistletoe*, 141.
35. Sparks, "Passion Tempered with Patience."
36. Quinn, "The Talk of the Town."
37. Raffaelli, "Reinventing Retail," 3.
38. Morrison, "Arts Advocacy," in Morrison, *The Source of Self-Regard*, 64.
39. Raffaelli, "Reinventing Retail," 21.
40. Ibid., 41.
41. Carlyle, *On Heroes, Hero-Worship, and the Heroic in History*, 22–23.
42. Musil, *Precision and Soul*, 132.
43. Quoted in Ordine, *The Usefulness of the Useless*, 85.
44. Quoted in Bialik and Ravnitzky, *The Book of Legends*, 408.
45. Quoted in ibid., 406.
46. Quoted in ibid., 403.
47. Avot 2:8.
48. Flexner, *The Usefulness of Useless Knowledge*, 5.
49. Ibid., 5 (emphasis added).
50. Ibid., 16–17.
51. Ibid., 36–37.
52. Ibid., 57.
53. Ibid., 60.
54. Ordine, *The Usefulness of the Useless*, 26.
55. Cioran, *Drawn and Quartered*, 82.
56. Olson, *Chicago Renaissance*, 15.
57. Ruskin, "Unto This Last," in Ruskin, *Unto This Last and Other Writings*, 168.

CHAPTER FOUR. COMMUNITY

1. James, "On Some Omissions of Introspective Psychology," in James, *Essays in Psychology*, 143.
2. Simic, "Reading Philosophy at Night," 141.
3. Stevens, "The House Was Quiet and the World Was Calm," in Stevens, *Collected Poetry and Prose*, 312.
4. Wright, *Black Boy*, 273.

5. Quoted in Doherty and Kwong, *If You Weren't Looking for It*, 74.
6. Quoted in ibid., 42, 74.
7. Jamie Kalven generously allowed me access to his private papers, including his notes for a book on the Seminary Co-op and its community. All Kalven references are from the papers, unless otherwise noted.
8. Whitman, "Song of the Open Road, 6," in Whitman, *Poetry and Prose*, 301.
9. Kalven, "Browsing in the Labyrinth."
10. Morley, *John Mistletoe*, 289.
11. Kalven, "Browsing in the Labyrinth."
12. Hyde, *The Gift*, 56.
13. Kenkō, *Essays in Idleness*, 12.
14. Quoted in Jackson, *The Anatomy of Bibliomania*, 86.
15. Quoted in ibid., 169.
16. Hazlitt, *Literary Remains of the Late William Hazlitt*, lvi.
17. Quoted in Leonard, *The Booklovers' Anthology*, 3.
18. Ruefle, *Madness, Rack, and Honey*, 206.
19. Quoted in Leonard, *The Booklovers' Anthology*, 1–2.
20. Ibid., 2.
21. Hunt, "My Books," in Hunt, *The World of Books and Other Essays*, 17.
22. Calvino, *The Uses of Literature*, 130.
23. Quoted in Jackson, *The Anatomy of Bibliomania*, 89.
24. Quoted in ibid., 85.
25. Ibid., 89.
26. Kenkō, *Essays in Idleness*, 12.
27. Hazlitt, *Literary Remains of the Late William Hazlitt*, lvi.
28. Emerson, "The American Scholar," in Emerson, *Essays and Lectures*, 58.
29. Ibid., 57–58.
30. Calvino, *Six Memos for the Next Millennium*, 114–15.
31. Hunt, "My Books," in Hunt, *The World of Books and Other Essays*, 40.
32. Whitman, "Poets to Come," in Whitman, *Poetry and Prose*, 175.
33. Ibid., 992–93.
34. Buber, *I and Thou*, 62.
35. Quoted in Doherty and Kwong, *If You Weren't Looking for It*, 52.
36. Abdurraqib, *They Can't Kill Us Until They Kill Us*, 7.
37. Miller, *Conversation*, 90.
38. Phillips and Taylor, *On Kindness*, 51.

39. Shils, "The Bookstore in America," 93.
40. Turkle, *Reclaiming Conversation*, 332.
41. Kalven Committee, "Report on the University's Role in Political and Social Action"; UChicago Architecture, "Stanley Tigerman on the Seminary Co-op Bookstore."
42. Quoted in Doherty and Kwong, *If You Weren't Looking for It*, 123.

CHAPTER FIVE. TIME

1. Seneca, *Epistulae Morales*, 3–5.
2. Musil, *The Man without Qualities*, 265.
3. Hardwick, "Reflections on Fiction," in Hardwick, *The Collected Essays of Elizabeth Hardwick*, 174.
4. Ibid.
5. Cappello, *Lecture*, 21.
6. Augustine, *Confessions*, 6.
7. Hardwick, "Reflections on Fiction," in Hardwick, *The Collected Essays of Elizabeth Hardwick*, 174.
8. Kundera, *Slowness*, 39.
9. Ibid., 3.
10. Emerson, "Education," in Emerson, *Lectures and Biographical Sketches*, 155.
11. Smith, *Intimations*, 22.
12. Quinn, "The Talk of the Town."
13. Shakespeare, *King Lear*, 108.
14. Benjamin, *Illuminations*, 61.
15. Proverbs 15:23.
16. Klein, *The Secret Pulse of Time*, 16.
17. Conrad, "The Nigger of the 'Narcissus,'" in Conrad, *Conrad's Prefaces to His Works*, 50.
18. Calvino, *The Uses of Literature*, 132.
19. Valéry, *Analects*, 10.
20. Calvino, *Six Memos for the Next Millennium*, 124.
21. Conrad, "The Nigger of the 'Narcissus,'" in Conrad, *Conrad's Prefaces to His Works*, 50.
22. Musil, *Precision and Soul*, 239.
23. Calvino, *Why Read the Classics?*, 241.
24. Borges, "The Garden of Forking Paths," in Borges, *Labyrinths*, 28.
25. Carlyle, *On Heroes, Hero-Worship, and the Heroic in History*, 148.
26. Carruthers, "Mechanisms for the Transmission of Culture," 6.

27. Calvino, *The Uses of Literature*, 132.
28. Emerson, "Experience," in Emerson, *Essays and Lectures*, 471.
29. Lispector, *Água Viva*, 16.
30. Hippocrates, *Hippocrates*, vol. IV, 495.
31. Weil, *Gravity and Grace*, 174.
32. Augustine, *Confessions*, 378.
33. Stevens, "Le Monocle de Mon Oncle," in Stevens, *Collected Poetry and Prose*, 11–13.
34. Weil, *Gravity and Grace*, 161.
35. Bialik and Ravnitzky, *The Book of Legends*, 762.
36. Borges, "The Garden of Forking Paths," in Borges, *Labyrinths*, 20.
37. Bachelard, *The Intuition of the Instant*, 8.
38. Valéry, *Analects*, 265.
39. Ibid., 307.
40. Ibid., 605.
41. Hyde, *The Gift*, 151.
42. Bachelard, *The Intuition of the Instant*, 3–4.
43. Conrad, "The Nigger of the 'Narcissus,'" in Conrad, *Conrad's Prefaces to His Works*, 54.
44. Joubert, *Pensées and Letters of Joseph Joubert*, 151.
45. Lispector, *Água Viva*, 68.
46. Robinson, *What Are We Doing Here?*, 113.
47. Valéry, *Analects*, 532.
48. Whitman, *Democratic Vistas*, in Whitman, *Poetry and Prose*, 952.
49. Shabbat, 34b.
50. Pesachim, 54b.
51. Dillard, *The Writing Life*, 72–73.
52. Conrad, "The Nigger of the 'Narcissus,'" in Conrad, *Conrad's Prefaces to His Works*, 52.
53. Ibid.

THE GOOD BOOKSTORE: AN EPILOGUE

1. Gopnik, "When a Bookstore Closes, an Argument Ends."
2. Stavans, *Borges, the Jew*, x.
3. Hardwick, "Reading, 16.
4. Borges, "On Exactitude in Science," in Borges, *Collected Fictions*, 325.
5. Robinson, *When I Was a Child I Read Books*, 22–23.

BIBLIOGRAPHY

Abdurraqib, Hanif. 2017. *They Can't Kill Us Until They Kill Us*. Columbus, OH: Two Dollar Radio.

Augustine. 2018. *Confessions*. New York: Modern Library.

Bachelard, Gaston. 2013. *The Intuition of the Instant*. Evanston, IL: Northwestern University Press.

———. 2014. *The Poetics of Space*, translated by Maria Jolas. New York: Penguin Classics.

Bacon, Francis. 1838. *Of the Proficience and Advancement of Learning*. London: William Pickering.

Barnes, Jonathan, ed. 1984. *The Complete Works of Aristotle*. Princeton, NJ: Princeton University Press.

Battles, Matthew. 2011. *Library: An Unquiet History*. New York: W. W. Norton & Co.

Benjamin, Walter. 1969. *Illuminations: Essays and Reflections*. New York: Schocken Books.

Bialik, Hayim Nahman, and Yehoshua Hana Ravnitzky, eds. 1992. *The Book of Legends: Sefer Ha-Aggadah*. New York: Schocken Books.

Bishop, Elizabeth. 2011. *Poems*. New York: Farrar, Straus and Giroux.

Blake, William. 1988. *The Complete Poetry and Prose of William Blake*. New York: Anchor Books.

The Booksellers' League. 1905. *The Booksellers' League: A History of Its Formation and Ten Years of Its Work*. New York: The Booksellers' League.

Borges, Jorge Luis. 1998. *Collected Fictions*. New York: Penguin Books.

———. 1964. *Labyrinths*. New York: New Directions.

———. 1999. *Selected Poems*. New York: Viking.

Borges, Jorge Luis, Edward Hirsch, Alastair Reid, Ben Belitt, Norman Thomas Di Giovanni, W. S. Merwin, Richard Howard, César Rennert, and John Updike. 1998. "Poetry: Jorge Luis Borges." *Wilson Quarterly* 22 (4): 109–14.

Brooks, Gwendolyn. 1983. *Very Young Poets*. Chicago: Brooks Press.

Buber, Martin. 1970. *I and Thou*. New York: Charles Scribner's Sons.

Burton, Robert. 1927. *The Anatomy of Melancholy*. New York: Tudor Publishing.

Calvino, Italo. 1988. *Six Memos for the Next Millennium*. New York: Vintage International.

———. 1986. *The Uses of Literature*. San Diego: Harcourt Brace Jovanovich.

———. 1999. *Why Read the Classics?* New York: Vintage Books.

Canetti, Elias. 1994. *The Agony of Flies: Notes and Notations*. New York: Farrar, Straus and Giroux.

Cappello, Mary. 2020. *Lecture*. Oakland, CA: Transit Books.

Carlyle, Thomas. 1895. *On Heroes, Hero-Worship, and the Heroic in History*. London: Chapman and Hall.

Carruthers, Mary. 2008. "Mechanisms for the Transmission of Culture: The Role of 'Place' in the Arts of Memory." In *Translatio: The Transmission of Culture in the Middle Ages and the Renaissance: Modes and Messages*, edited by Laura H. Hollengreen, 1–26. Turnhout, Belgium: Brepols.

Carter, Steven D., ed. 2014. *The Columbia Anthology of Japanese Essays*. New York: Columbia University Press.

Cicero. 1970. *Orations: Pro Caelio, De provinciis consularibus, Pro Balbo*. Cambridge, MA: Harvard University Press.

Cioran, E. M. 1983. *Drawn and Quartered*. New York: Arcade Publishing.

Cole, John Y. 1981. *Responsibilities of the American Book Community*. Washington, DC: Library of Congress.

Conrad, Joseph. 1937. *Conrad's Prefaces to His Works*. New York: Haskell House.

de Bury, Richard. 1948. *The Philobiblon*. Berkeley: University of California Press.

Dillard, Annie. 1990. *The Writing Life*. New York: HarperPerennial.

Doherty, Megan E., and Jasmine Kwong. 2016. *If You Weren't Looking for It: The Seminary Co-op Bookstore*. Chicago: Self-published.

Donne, John. 1958. *The Sermons of John Donne*. New York: Meridian Books.

Emerson, Ralph Waldo. 1983. *Essays and Lectures*, edited by Joel Porte. New York: Library of America.

———. 1904. *Lectures and Biographical Sketches*. Boston: Houghton Mifflin.

———. 1883. *Society and Solitude*. Boston: Houghton Mifflin.

Epicurus. 1993. *The Essential Epicurus*. Amherst, NY: Prometheus Books.

Flexner, Abraham. 2017. *The Usefulness of Useless Knowledge*. Companion essay by Robbert Dijkgraaf. Princeton, NJ: Princeton University Press.

Gandhi, Mohandas K. 1993. *An Autobiography: The Story of My Experiments with Truth*. Boston: Beacon Press.

Gissing, George. 1903. *The Private Papers of Henry Ryecroft*. Westminster: Archibald Constable & Co.

Gopnik, Adam. 2015. "When a Bookstore Closes, an Argument Ends." *New Yorker*, June 12. https://www.newyorker.com/news/daily -comment/when-a-bookstore-closes-an-argument-ends (accessed January 30, 2020).

Grothaus, Michael. 2019. "A Rediscovered 1997 Video Reveals Why Jeff Bezos Chose Books and Not CDs to Be Amazon's First Product." *Fast Company*, November 13. https://www.fastcompany .com/90430303/a-rediscovered-1997-video-reveals-why-jeff-bezos -chose-books-and-not-cds-to-be-amazons-first-product (accessed January 30, 2020).

Gupta, Gargi. 2014. "A Bookstore with a Difference." *DNA India*, January 26. https://www.dnaindia.com/lifestyle/interview-a -bookstore-with-a-difference-1957196 (accessed January 31, 2021).

Hardwick, Elizabeth. 2017. *The Collected Essays of Elizabeth Hardwick*. New York: New York Review Books.

———. 1983. "Reading." *Daedalus* 112 (1): 13–18.

Hazlitt, William. 1836. *Literary Remains of the Late William Hazlitt: With a Notice of His Life*. London: Saunders and Otley.

Hippocrates. 1998. *Hippocrates*, vol. IV, translated by W.H.S. Jones. Cambridge, Mass.: Harvard University Press.

Hunt, Leigh. 1899. *The World of Books and Other Essays*. London: Gay and Bird.

Hyde, Lewis. 1983. *The Gift: Imagination and the Erotic Life of Property*. New York: Vintage Books.

Jackson, Holbrook. 2001. *The Anatomy of Bibliomania*. Champaign: University of Illinois Press.

James, William. 1983. "On Some Omissions of Introspective Psychology." in *Essays in Psychology*. Cambridge, MA: Harvard University Press.

Jewett, Charles C. 1846. *The Facts and Considerations Relative to the Duties on Books*. Providence, RI: J. F. Moore.

Joubert, Joseph. 1928. *Pensées and Letters of Joseph Joubert*. London: George Routledge & Sons, Ltd.

Kalven Committee. 1967. "Report on the University's Role in Political and Social Action." Chicago: University of Chicago (November 11). https://provost.uchicago.edu/sites/default/files/documents/reports/KalvenRprt_0.pdf (accessed February 18, 2020).

Kalven, Jamie. 1991. "Browsing in the Labyrinth." *University of Chicago Magazine* (December): 20–25.

Kawaguchi, Karen. 2000. "Feminist Feast and Famine." *Publishers Weekly*, July 24.

Kenkō. 1967. *Essays in Idleness: The Tzurezuregusa of Kenkō*, translated by Donald Keene. New York: Columbia University Press.

Klein, Stefan. 2006. *The Secret Pulse of Time: Making Sense of Life's Scarcest Commodity*. New York: Marlowe & Co.

Kundera, Milan. 2014. *Slowness: A Novel*. New York: HarperPerennial.

Laertius, Diogenes. 1972. *Lives of Eminent Philosophers*. Cambridge, MA: Harvard University Press.

Lamb, Charles. 1885. *The Essays of Elia*. New York: A. L. Burt, Publisher.

Leonard, R. M., ed. 2016. *The Booklovers' Anthology: A Compendium of Writing about Books, Readers, and Libraries*. Oxford: Bodleian Library.

Lessing, Doris. 1999. *The Golden Notebook*. New York: HarperPerennial.

Lispector, Clarice. 2012. *Água Viva*. New York: New Directions.

Liu, An. 2010. *The Huainanzi*. New York: Columbia University Press.

Locke, John. 1912. *Of the Conduct of the Understanding* [1706]. In *The Educational Writings of John Locke*. New York: Longmans, Green & Co.

London Library. 2016. *On Reading, Writing, and Living with Books*. London: Pushkin Press.

Lowell, James Russell. 1871. *Among My Books*. Boston: Fields, Osgood, & Co.

Macaulay, Rose. 1936. *Personal Pleasures*. New York: Macmillan.

Manguel, Alberto. 1997. *A History of Reading*. New York: Penguin Books.

———. 2018. *Packing My Library: An Elegy and Ten Digressions*. New Haven, CT: Yale University Press.

McColvin, Lionel. 1933. *How to Use Books*. London: Cambridge University Press.

Melville, Herman. 1992. *Moby-Dick, or, The Whale*. New York: Penguin Classics.

Mencken, H. L. 1930. "Lo, the Poor Bookseller." *American Mercury* (October).

Miller, Stephen. 2006. *Conversation: A History of a Declining Art*. New Haven, CT: Yale University Press.

Montaigne, Michel de. 1958. *The Complete Essays of Montaigne*, translated by Donald M. Frame. Stanford, CA: Stanford University Press.

Morley, Christopher. 1931. *John Mistletoe*. London: Faber and Faber.

Morrison, Toni. 2019. *The Source of Self-Regard: Selected Essays, Speeches, and Meditations*. New York: Alfred A. Knopf.

Musil, Robert. 1995. *The Man without Qualities*. New York: Vintage International.

———. 1990. *Precision and Soul: Essays and Addresses*. Chicago: University of Chicago Press.

Nancy, Jean-Luc. 2009. *On the Commerce of Thinking: On Books and Bookstores*, translated by David Wills. New York: Fordham University Press.

———. 2009. "Bookseller." In *The Encyclopedia of Diderot and d'Alembert Collaborative Translation Project*, translated by Audra Merfeld-Langston. Ann Arbor: Michigan Publishing, University of Michigan Library. http://hdl.handle.net/2027/spo.did2222.0001 .039 (accessed August 8, 2021). Originally published as "Librairie," in *Encyclopédie ou Dictionnaire raisonné des sciences, des arts et des métiers*, 9:478 (Paris, 1765).

Nawotka, Ed. 2020. "ABA Added 111 Stores in 2019." *Publishers Weekly*, January 30.

O'Brien, Geoffrey. 2000. *The Browser's Ecstasy: A Meditation on Reading*. New York: Counterpoint.

Okakura, Kakuzō. 2010. *The Book of Tea*. New York: Penguin Classics.

Olson, Liesl. 2017. *Chicago Renaissance: Literature and Art in the Midwest Metropolis*. New Haven, CT: Yale University Press.

Ordine, Nuccio. 2017. *The Usefulness of the Useless*, translated by Alastair McEwen. Philadelphia: Paul Dry Books.

Perec, Georges. 1997. *Species of Spaces and Other Pieces*. New York: Penguin Classics.

Phillips, Adam, and Barbara Taylor. 2009. *On Kindness*. New York: Farrar, Straus and Giroux.

Pound, Ezra. 1951. *ABC of Reading*. New York: New Directions.

Quignard, Pascal. 2018. *The Roving Shadows*. London: Seagull Books.

Quinn, Alice. 1988. "The Talk of the Town." *New Yorker*, January 25, 25–26.

Raffaelli, Ryan. 2020. "Reinventing Retail: The Novel Resurgence of Independent Bookstores." Working Paper. Boston: Harvard Business School (January).

Ranganathan, S. R. 2006. *The Five Laws of Library Science*. New Delhi: Ess Ess Publications.

Richardson, Robert. 2009. *First We Read, Then We Write: Emerson on the Creative Drive*. Iowa City: University of Iowa Press.

Robinson, Marilynne. 2018. *What Are We Doing Here? Essays*. New York: Farrar, Straus and Giroux.

———. 2012. *When I Was a Child I Read Books: Essays*. New York: Farrar, Straus and Giroux.

Ruefle, Mary. 2012. *Madness, Rack, and Honey: Collected Lectures*. Seattle: Wave Books.

Ruskin, John. 2002. *Sesame and Lilies*. New Haven, CT: Yale University Press.

———. 1997. *Unto This Last and Other Writings*. New York: Penguin Classics.

Schenden, Gregory. 2018. "Entering the Thin Places." *The Hoya*, March 19.

Schonwald, Josh. 2001. "The Seminary Co-op Turns Another Page." *University of Chicago Magazine* (December).

Seneca. 1967. *Epistulae Morales*. Cambridge, MA: Harvard University Press.

Shakespeare, William. 2009. *King Lear*. New York: Modern Library.

Shils, Edward. 1963. "The Bookstore in America." *Daedalus* 112 (Winter): 92–104.

Silver, Sean. 2015. "The Prehistory of Serendipity, from Bacon to Walpole." *Isis* 106 (June): 235–56.

Simic, Charles. 1990. "Reading Philosophy at Night." In *Antaeus: Literature as Pleasure*, edited by Daniel Halpern, 135–42. London: Collins Harvill.

Smith, Zadie. 2020. *Intimations: Six Essays*. New York: Penguin Books.

Sontag, Susan. 2012. *As Consciousness Is Harnessed to Flesh: Journals and Notebooks, 1964–1980*. New York: Farrar, Straus and Giroux.

Sparks, Stephen. 2017. "Passion Tempered with Patience: An Interview with Paul Yamazaki." *ZYZZYVA* (Fall).

Stavans, Ilan. 2016. *Borges, the Jew*. Albany: State University of New York Press.

Stevens, Wallace. 1996. *Collected Poetry and Prose*. New York: Library of America.

Thoreau, Henry David. 1986. *Walden and Civil Disobedience*. New York: Penguin Classics.

Turkle, Sherry. 2015. *Reclaiming Conversation: The Power of Talk in a Digital Age*. New York: Penguin Press.

UChicago Architecture. 2013. "Stanley Tigerman on the Seminary Co-op Bookstore." Posted on YouTube, November 11. https://www.youtube.com/watch?v=FIp6s4n2URg (accessed January 30, 2020).

Valéry, Paul. 1970. *Analects*, vol. 14 of *Collected Works of Paul Valéry*. Princeton, NJ: Princeton University Press.

Weil, Simone. 1997. *Gravity and Grace*. Lincoln: University of Nebraska Press.

Weinberger, Eliot. 2016. *The Ghosts of Birds: Essays*. New York: New Directions.

Whitman, Walt. 1982. *Poetry and Prose*. New York: Library of America.

Woolf, Virginia. 1960. *The Second Common Reader*. New York: Harcourt Brace Jovanovich.

———. 2005. *To the Lighthouse*. Boston: Mariner Books.

Wright, Richard. 1963. *Black Boy*. New York: Harper & Brothers.

Zaid, Gabriel. 2003. *So Many Books: Reading and Publishing in an Age of Abundance*. Philadelphia: Paul Dry Books.

INDEX

ABC of Reading (Pound), 69

Abdul Kassem Ismael, Grand Vizier of Persia, 30

abundance: and necessity of filtration and selection, 56–57, 67–68; number of books published, 51, 65–67; time required to read entire collections, 62–64; totalizing, 60; and use, 55; and weeding, 68–69

adjacency: and browsing, 46–47; and classification of books, 41–42, 44; and discovery, 38, 41–42, 51; and meaning, 46–47; in time, 145–146; and Warburg's Law of the Good Neighbor, 51, 79

advice. *See* recommendations

Alighieri, Dante, 105–106

Amazon, 6–7, 9, 82, 87–89, 99

American Booksellers Association (ABA), 96–97

anthologies, bookstores as, 22

apikores (heretics), 121–122

Aristotle, 28

arrangement of books, 51; alphabetical schemes for, 30–31, 40–42, 73; as composition, 70–71; Front Tables, 69–71, 127, 139–140. *See also* adjacency

Augustine, Saint, 139

Bachelard, Gaston, 20, 30, 154, 156, 163

Bacon, Francis, 13–14

Baker, Nicholson, 49

Baldwin, James, 81–82

Benjamin, Walter, 55n, 143

Bentham, Jeremy, 100–101

Bessarione, Cardinal, 79

Beth Medrash Govoha, Lakewood, 102–103

Bezos, Jeff, 6–7. *See also* Amazon

"Bibliography (The Cloud Bookcase)" (Weinberger), 43

Bishop, Elizabeth, 60

Blake, William, 60, 137

blindness, 65–66

Bnei Yehuda, Brooklyn, 120

Bodleian Library, Oxford, 12–13

The Book of Tea (Okakura), 80

books: Amazon's devaluing of, 6–7, 82, 87–89, 99; as commodities, 3, 6–7, 64, 84, 93–95, 98, 142–143; as companions, 117–119, 148; as manuals for living, 77, 125; ownership of, 52–53, 75–76, 128–129; shelf

books (*continued*)
life of books as products, 64, 94–95, 98, 142–143; and the unknown, 58–59; unread, 55–56, 59; use as purpose of, 50, 66, 75–76; wisdom in, 78–79

booksellers: as builders of bookstores, 8–9, 17, 51, 56, 165, 167; as community builders, 17, 131; and conversation, 115–116; cultural role and influence of, 7, 17, 79; and discerning selection of books, 4, 51, 55–56, 67–68, 79, 91 (*see also* filtration); and ethos of service, 113–114; and gift labors, 89–90, 142; as hosts, 61–62; and human connections, 115–116; media conglomerates as, 91–92; as merchants, 86–89; motivation and vocation of, 5–6, 9, 15–16, 48n; as "professors of books," 69; qualities required in professional, 69–71, 73–74, 115–116; as readers, 15–16, 135–136; and recommendation of books, 32–33, 57, 71–74, 159–160; time as understood and respected by, 50–51, 116, 142–143, 159–160; as unobtrusive, 37, 113–114, 119; wages for, 98–99

"The Bookshop in America" (Shils), 1–2, 6, 8

bookstores: as assembled or built by booksellers, 8–9, 17, 51, 56, 165, 167; browsing experience as product of, 24–29, 33, 166 (*see also* browsing); as catalogs of catalogs, 164–165; and community, 17–18, 77, 111–112, 115, 130–131; as democratic, egalitarian institutions, 126–132, 134; as encyclopedias, 22; and "everything stores," 6, 68; as gifts, 115–116; inventories as collections, 4, 6, 22, 68–69, 91, 122, 157; libraries contrasted with, 52–53, 128; literary forms akin to, 21–24, 59n; open air markets and bookstalls, 76; and permission to encounter books, 12–13; as physical spaces (*see* space); and privacy of patrons, 114–116; as public good, 33, 38, 111, 128; as retail businesses (*see* market economy); as sanctified or sacred places, 129; as scarce, 95–96; as sites of learning, 12–13; *vs.* storehouses of books, 53, 56–57; as storehouses of memory, 147; as "thin places" with access to heaven, 47–48; as totalizing environments, 9–10, 22, 81, 133; value of, 32–34, 166

Booth, Wayne, 122

Borges, Jorge Luis, 1, 18, 40, 44–45, 64–65, 71, 74, 146–147, 154; and Judaism, 163–165

Boro Park, 10, 18

Bouvard and Pécuchet (Flaubert), 59, 125

Brooks, Gwendolyn, 109

browsers: as *chefs*, 26, 143; as *connoisseurs*, 27–28; customer service needs of, 71–72, 113–114; as *devotees*, 26; as *flaneurs*, 26, 36; as *generals*, 26–27, 54–55, 62, 73; as *idlers*, 27, 36; indiscriminate, 57; as *initiates*, 26, 54, 61–62; as *palimpsests*, 26; as *penitents*, 26; as *pilgrims*, 26, 36–37, 54–55, 61; privacy and anonymity of, 114–116; as ruminators, 26 (*see also* rumination); *as sandpipers*, 26, 60, 156; as *stargazers*, 26, 47; as *town criers*, 26

browsing: and absence of distractions, 37; and discovery, 32–37, 58–59, 75, 139–140; and disorientation, 20–21; etymology and definition of term, 24–25; experience as product of bookstores, 9, 20, 24–29, 33, 113–114, 166; and intuition, 36–37, 58, 112–113; pleasure grounds for, 31–32, 142, 144, 156; and rumination, 17–18, 23–28, 37–38, 138–139, 144–148; and serendipity, 35–36, 38; shelving and (*see* adjacency); taxonomies and (*see* classification of books); time required for, 139–141, 144–146, 149–150; types of bookstore browsers (*see* browsers); voids and, 45–46; and wandering, 27–28, 130–131; wisdom as reward for, 34–35

Buber, Martin, 127

Burton, Robert, 15

business finance. *See* market economy

Calvino, Italo, 51, 59, 75–77, 122, 128–129, 144–145, 146, 148

Canetti, Elias, 75, 140n

canons: booksellers as influence on, 79, 94–95; personal, 55, 75–77, 122, 164

Cappello, Mary, 21–22, 138–139

Carlyle, Thomas, 79–80, 100, 147

Carruthers, Mary, 147

Carter, Steven, 24

cataloging. *See* classification of books

catalogs: booksellers and use of publishers', 67–68, 73–74; bookstores as, 164–165; and discovery, 71–74

Cella, Jack, 8–9, 20, 39, 164–165

chefs, 26, 143

chevrusa, 11–12, 120, 122, 131

Cicero, 78

Cioran, E. M., 106

City Lights Booksellers, San Francisco, 43, 44, 48, 95

"classics" enduring books "of all time," 3–4, 79, 94, 116, 148, 149, 166; and publishing industry time table, 93

classification of books: academic conventions for, 42–43; and adjacencies, 39, 41–42, 44; alphabetical schemes for, 30–31, 40–42, 73; as arbitrary but internally logical, 40, 44–45; by booksellers, 42–43; catalogers as ordainers of the universe, 39; "catalogue of catalogues" and, 71–74, 164–165; chaos and, 73–74; as expression of bookstore's

classification of books (*continued*)
   philosophy, 42–43; Perec
   on, 38–39; reclassification,
   44–45; as tyrannical, 45
collections, bookstore inventories as assembled, 4, 6, 22,
   69, 91, 122, 157
commonplace books, bookstores
   as, 23
community: and bookstores,
   17–18, 77, 111–112, 115,
   130–131; bookstores as
   public good, 33, 38, 111,
   128; *chevrusa* and community of learning, 11–12,
   120–121; cooperatives and,
   33; and gift economy, 115;
   Kalven on bookstores and,
   111–112, 130–131; and kindness, 130–131; and loneliness,
   145; patrons of bookstores
   as, 55–56, 111–112; personal
   canons as, 122, 164; and
   solitude, 109–110, 116, 120
Confessions (Augustine), 139,
   150
connoisseurs, 27–28
Conrad, Joseph, 85–86,
   143–144, 156, 159–160
conversation: books as partners
   in, 117, 120–122, 125–126;
   bookselling as, 115–116;
   bookstores as places for,
   109, 131–135, 166; culture as,
   76–77; reading as, 3–4, 110,
   117, 120, 122; and respect,
   131–132
Conversation (Miller), 129–130
Co-op Bookstore, Chicago. *See*
   Seminary Cooperative Bookstore, Inc.

culture: bookstores and cultivation of literary, 76–77,
   135–136, 147; democratizing
   spaces and literary, 129–130;
   economics and, 83–84,
   106–107; investment in,
   83–84; universality and diversity of, 76–77; value of, 83
curation. *See* filtration

daf yomi, 120
Dante Alighieri, 105–106
Davis, Lydia, vi
de Bury, Richard, vi, 78–79, 91
"Democratic Vistas" (Whitman),
   126–127
de Tocqueville, Alexis, 102,
   104–105
devotees, 26
Dijkgraaf, Robbert, 104
Dillard, Annie, 158–159
Dillingham, Charles, 2, 15
Diogenes Laertius, 28
discovery: and adjacencies, 38,
   41–42, 51; algorithms for,
   32–33; and browsing, 32–33,
   58–59, 75, 139–140; catalogs
   and, 71–74; and number of
   books available, 57–58; and
   presence as persuasion, 18;
   and recommendations or
   advice, 32–33, 52–53, 57,
   71–75, 74–75, 113–114; and
   relationships among books,
   74–75; as rescue of the book,
   45; and serendipity, 35–36,
   38; time required for, 140
distraction, avoidance of, 37,
   109, 114
Doctorow, E. L., 91
Doniger, Wendy, 39, 44

Donne, John, 50
Dryden, John, 24–25

Ecclesiastes, 56
economics. See gift economy;
    market economy
efficiency, 3, 16–17, 27, 32, 80,
    92, 96, 137–139, 141
Emerson, Ralph Waldo, 57–58,
    63, 69, 124–125, 127, 142,
    149
encyclopedias and encyclo-
    pedism, 2, 22, 59–60, 125;
    human life as, 77, 109, 116
enthusiasm, 4, 6, 15, 91, 109,
    116, 136, 157; and book cul-
    ture, 136; of booksellers, 4,
    6, 15, 76, 91, 157–158
ephemera and the ephemeral, 14,
    24, 57, 91, 141, 144, 159–160;
    "books of the hour," 3–4,
    93–94, 116, 148, 149, 166
Epicurus, 28–29, 121, 131
essays, bookstores as, 22–23
ethics, 101, 106–108
Ewing, Eve, 148
"Experience" (Emerson), 149

The Facts and Considerations
    Relative to the Duties on
    Books (Jewett), 65–66
Faraday, Michael, 105
filtration: abundance of books
    and necessity for, 55–57,
    67–68; booksellers and, 4,
    6, 46, 56, 72, 91, 135, 157;
    publishers' catalogs and,
    67–68, 73–74; and weeding or
    pruning, 68–69
financial models. See gift
    economy; market economy

"Five Laws of Library Science"
    (Ranganathan), 50
flaneurs, 26, 36
Flaubert, Gustave, 59, 125
Flexner, Abraham, 104–105
Forster, E. M., 56
Front Tables, 69–71, 127,
    139–140

Gandhi, Mohandas, 86
Gaos, José, 76
"The Garden of Forking Paths"
    (Borges), 146–147
Gautier, Théophile, 84
generals, 26–27, 54–55, 62, 73
gift economy, 85–86, 90, 114–115;
    and book culture, 160–161;
    and bookselling as labor in,
    89–90, 142; and human con-
    nections, 115; and kindness
    or generosity, 130; and time,
    142, 160–161
The Gift (Hyde), 85–87, 90
Gissing, George, 84
Gopnik, Adam, 162
Gotham Book Mart, New York, 95
Gravity and Grace (Weil), 150–151
Gray Wolf Books, San Leandro, 56

Hardwick, Elizabeth, 138,
    140–141, 164
Hazlitt, William, 117, 123
Heinsius, Daniël, 14–15
"Helpless Europe" (Musil), 101,
    137–138, 145
Hemon, Aleksandar, 31, 77,
    80–81
Heraclitus, 34–35
heresy (apikores), 121–122
How to Use Books (McColvin), 66
Huainanzi (Lui), 22, 60

Hugo, Victor, 83
The Hungry Mind, St. Paul, 26
Hunt, Leigh, 11, 57, 119–120, 126
Hyde, Lewis, 85–86, 90, 114–115, 116, 142, 155

Ibn Tibbon, Samuel, 27–28
idleness, 15, 37–38
idlers, 27, 36
initiates, 26, 54, 61–62
Institute for Advanced Study (IAS), Princeton, 102, 104
interiority, 144–145
inventories of bookstores: as collections, 4, 6, 22, 69, 91, 122, 157
Ishiwara Masaakira, 24

Jackson, Holbrook, 123
James, William, 109
Janowitz, Morris, 111
Jerome, Saint, 84
Jewett, Charles Coffin, 65–66
Jirō, Osaragi, 41
John K. King Books, Detroit, 56
Jones, Alena, 46–47
Joubert, Joseph, 156
Judah bar Ilai, 102–103, 102–105

Kalven, Harry, Jr., 111, 133–135
Kalven, Jamie, 21–22, 114–115; and bookstore as community, 111–112, 130–131; and bookstore as literary form, 59n, 111–112; on public discourse and bookstores, 132–133
Kalven Report, University of Chicago, 133–135

Kenkō, 23–24, 117, 123, 157
kindness, 130–131, 158
kollels, 102–103
Kundera, Milan, 141–142

labor: study as labor for common good, 103–104; *vs.* work, 142
labyrinths, 29, 146–148
La Hune, Paris, 162
Lamb, Charles, 57, 119–120
Lear, Jonathan, 9, 31, 58, 70, 71–72
learning: books and, 12; Jewish reverence for, 10–12, 13, 102–107, 119–120, 164; as process requiring time, 142–143; and the unknowable, 158
Lessing, Doris, 74–75
Lessing, G. E., 25
libraries, 12–13; bookstores contrasted with, 52–53, 128; as growing organisms, 50; principles guiding, 133–134; as public institutions, 53; Ranganathan's "Five Laws of Library Science," 50; and "sideline services," 53
"The Library of Babel" (Borges), 1, 40, 71, 74
Lispector, Clarice, 150, 156
"Lo, the Poor Bookseller" (Mencken), 4–5
loss leaders, 6–7, 87–88, 99
Lowell, James Russell, 24–25

Macaulay, Rose, 68
Machiavelli, Niccolò, 117
Manguel, Alberto, 30, 39, 45, 51
The Man without Qualities (Musil), 35–36, 54, 59

market economy (bookstores as retail businesses), 1–2; and academic books, 98; and books as commodities, 3, 6–7, 64, 84, 93–95, 98, 142–143; and cooperative financial model, 33; and devaluation of books, 6–7, 82, 87–88, 99; and efficiency, 16–17, 32, 80; failed economic models, 32–33, 90–91, 99–100; and gift economy, 114–115; and loss leaders as strategy, 6–7, 87–88, 99; pricing considerations, 78–79, 87–89; and profitability, 8, 32–34, 96–100; and shelf-life of books, 64, 94–95, 98, 142–143; and sidelines, 5–6, 9, 96, 98–99; stocking decisions and, 57–58; and 3C's, 96; and value *vs.* profit, 32–34. *See also* publishers

"The Marriage of Heaven and Hell" (Blake), 137

Marshall, Nate, 12

Mayer, Peter, 93–94

McColvin, Lionel, 66, 81

McNally, Sarah, 165

McNally Jackson Books, New York, 43

meaning: bookstores and, 8, 29, 37, 46–47, 100–101, 127, 131–132, 148–149, 161, 162; learning and, 8, 12–13; reading and narrative, 127

Melville, Herman, 60–61, 153n

memory, 109, 141, 147, 159

Mencken, H. L., 4–5

Miller, Stephen, 129–130

Miriam's well, 153

Moby Dick (Melville), 60–61, 153n

Modschiedler, John, 8

Moe's Bookstore, Berkeley, 48

"Le Monocle de Mon Oncle" (Stevens), 150–151

Montaigne, Michel de, 19, 22, 128n

Morley, Christopher, vi, 5, 27, 55, 92, 94–95, 114

Morrison, Toni, 95, 97

Musil, Robert, 35–36, 54, 59, 62, 85, 101

Nancy, Jean-Luc, 16, 162

National Library of Argentina, 64–65

O'Brien, Geoffrey, 59, 73–74

"Of Books" (Montaigne), 19

Okakura, Kakuzō, 80

Olson, Liesl, 106

"On Exactitude in Science" (Borges), 165

On the Commerce of Thinking (Nancy), 162

Ordine, Nuccio, 83

palimpsests, 26

penitents, 26

Perec, Georges, 38–40

Personal Pleasures (Macaulay), 68

Pesachim, 152–153

Petrarch, 118, 122

Phillips, Adam, 130

The Philobiblon (de Bury), 78–79

Phinney Books, Seattle, 43

pilgrims, 26, 36–37, 54–55, 61

"Poem of the Gifts" (Borges), 64–65

The Poetics of Space (Bachelard), 20
"Poets to Come" (Whitman), 126
Pound, Ezra, 69
Powell's Books, Portland, 48n, 111
presence of books, 9–10; booksellers and life in the, 48n; and bookstore arrangement, 41, 45–46 (*see also* adjacency); pillowbook tradition and, 23, 41. *See also* abundance
pricing books, 78–79, 87–89
"Pro Caelio" (Cicero), 78
profit. *See* market economy
proximity. *See* adjacency
publishers: and books as commodities, 93; catalogs, 67–68, 73–74; cultural role of, 92–39; and enduring books, 92–93; media conglomerates, 91–92; number of books in print, 3, 64; number of books published, 65–67; and time, 93

quiet, 37, 109–114, 119, 148, 150–151
Quignard, Pascal, 60, 84, 155

Raffaelli, Ryan, 96–99
Ranganathan, S. R., 50
readers: assimilation of books, 143–144; and book ownership, 52–53, 75–76; as booksellers promoting literary culture, 135–136; as changed by books, 26, 143–144; and his or her book, 50, 55, 95; and identity informed by books, 144, 148; and personal canons, 55, 75–77, 122, 164;

as specific community, 55–56, 122
reading: books as companions, 117–119, 148; booksellers as "readers of reading," 15–16; as both solitary and communal experience, 110; as conversation, 3–4, 110, 117, 120, 122; and critical thinking or self-examination, 132; as human connection, 126–127; quantifying reading life, 62–63, 121, 142–144; time and immersive or "slow," 137–138
recommendations, 52–53, 71–75, 113–114; algorithms to generate, 32–33; presence as persuasion, 18; and trust relationship with readers, 57
Renan, Ernest, 84
rereading, 75–76, 140n
Rilke, Rainer Maria, 143
Robinson, Marilynne, 38, 156–157, 165
Rousseau, Jean-Jacques, 83
Ruefle, Mary, 117
rumination: bookstores as spaces for, 17–18, 20–21, 30, 52, 155–156; browsing and, 17–18, 23–28, 37–38, 144–148, 166–167; time required for, 138–139, 145–148; and wandering, 27–28
Ruskin, John, 3, 34–35, 107–108; on merchants, 86–90

sandpipers, 26, 60, 156
scarcity, 80–81, 95–96
Schenden, Gregory, 47–48
Sei Shōnagon, 23

selection, booksellers and discerning, 4, 6, 16, 67–68; "barroom and bodega" inventory, 5, 92; profitability linked to, 98; weeding, 69–70

Seminary Cooperative Bookstore, Inc., Chicago, 7, 14–15, 48, 166–167; and browsing as physical experience, 9–10; Cella's role in building, 8–9, 20, 39, 164–165; mission statement of, 7, 28–29; relocation of, 18, 29–31; Tigerman and architecture of, 20–21, 39, 45–46, 71

Seneca, 137, 140

serendipity, 35–36, 38

"Sermon Preached at the Funeral of Sir William Cokayne" (Donne), 50

"Sesame and Lilies" (Ruskin), 3

Shammai the Elder, 103

shelf-life of books, 64, 94–99, 98, 142–143

shelving. See adjacency

Shils, Edward, 1–3, 6, 8, 15, 17, 57–58, 112n, 131

silence, 37, 109–114, 119, 148, 150–151

Silver, Sean, 35

Simic, Charles, 110, 127

Slowness (Kundera), 141–142

Smith, Zadie, 142

Socrates, 106

solitude, 109–111, 116, 120

Sontag, Susan, 76, 129

Source Booksellers, Detroit, 48

The Source of Self-Regard (Morrison), 97

space: architecture and browsing experience, 20–21, 39, 45–46, 71; and arrangement of books, 45–46 (see also adjacency); bookstores as sanctified spaces, 30–32; and browsing as primary activity, 20; and experience of time, 149; labyrinthine, 29, 146–148; "thick places," 48–49; "thin places," 47–48; use and cultural meaning, 29

Speed, Eldon, 68

stargazers, 26, 47

Stavans, Ilan, 163–164

Sterne, Laurence, 117

Stevens, Wallace, 39, 110, 150–151

Strand Books, New York, 46

Sunstein, Cass, 111

supply and demand. See abundance; scarcity

Tanhuma, 55, 152

Tatham, Edward H. R., 122

taxonomies: and bookstore identity, 39; and browsing, 39; types of bookstore patrons, 26–27; as tyrannical, 45. See also classification of books

Teicher, Oren, 96–98, 100

Tell Me How Long the Train's Been Gone (Baldwin), 81–82

Thomason, Edwin, 124

Thoreau, Henry David, 48–49

Tigerman, Stanley, 20–21, 39, 45–46, 71

time: and appreciation of the ephemeral, 18; booksellers and respect for readers' time, 50–51, 116; Borges and infinite, 146–147; for browsing, 139–141, 144–146, 149–150;

time (*continued*)
as compressed and dilated in bookstores, 145–146, 149, 153–154; and divine creation, 152–153; and efficiency, 137–139; experience of the present moment, 153–157; fiction and immersive experience of, 140–141; and gift economy, 142, 160–161; immersive or "slow," 138–139, 141–142, 159; and leisure, 144; and publishing industry, 93; quantifying time spent reading, 62–64, 121, 142–144; required to read entire collections, 62–64; respect for readers', 50–51; rumination and "slow time," 138–139, 145–148; space and experience of, 147; in the Talmud, 151–152; and uncertainty, 154–155; value of, 137–138
town criers, 26
Turkle, Sherry, 131–132
Turrell, James, 46

uncertainty: and browsing, 20–21; completeness and order, 40; and serendipity, 35–36; and time, 154–155, 157–159; voids and ambiguity, 46–47
use and purpose of books, 66; rereading, 75–76; utility of study, 102–104

Valéry, Paul, 144, 154, 157, 165n
value: "bargains" and, 78–79, 82, 91; books as investment, 81; of bookstores, 32–34, 166; commerce as devaluation, 105–106; cultural value of literature and study, 82, 106–107; de Bury on value of books, 78–79; devaluation of books, 6–7, 78–79, 82, 87–89, 99, 105–106; and gift economies, 89–90; quantification of, 100–101; scarcity and, 80–81; of study, 103–104, 106–107; of time, 137–138; of wisdom in books, 78–79; worth as distinct from, 107–108
Very Young Poets (Brooks), 109
voids: browsing and, 45–46; Turrell's Skyspaces as, 46; wisdom and, 34

Walpole, Horace, 35–36
Warburg, Aby, 51
Ward, Samuel Gray, 58
Warren, Kenneth, 31, 33–34
weeding, 68–70
Weil, Simone, 14, 123, 140, 150, 151
Weinberger, Eliot, 43
Whitman, Walt, 18, 85, 112, 126–127, 157
Woolf, Virginia, 75, 76, 159
Wright, Richard, 111

Yamazaki, Paul, 44, 95, 165
Yissachar-Zebulun partnership, 103–104, 106–107

Zaid, Gabriel, 64, 67
zuihitsu, 23–24, 41

A NOTE ON THE TYPE

This book has been composed in
Bookman Old Style and Job Clarendon.

Despite the "Old Style" in its name, Bookman lacks
the diagonal stress typical of old style letterforms;
rather, it is classified as a transitional serif typeface
for its near-vertical axis. The design is derived from
Old Style Antique, which was created by Alexander
Phemister around 1858 for the Scottish type foundry
Miller & Richard. From the mid-nineteenth through
early twentieth centuries, several American foundries
made versions of this type, which eventually became
known as Bookman. The digital version used here
was designed by Ong Chong Wah and first released
by Monotype in 1990.

Job Clarendon is a contemporary bracketed slab serif
typeface inspired by the condensed Clarendon styles
popular in nineteenth-century British and American
job printing. Designed by David Jonathan Ross in
collaboration with Bethany Heck, Job Clarendon was
released in ten upright weights as the March 2021
installment of Font of the Month Club.

Join us in supporting local independent bookstores.
Scan the code to find one near you.

press.princeton.edu/resources/bookstore-finder